packing and persevering

carry-on

scotty gibbons

Carry-On
Packing and Persevering for Success in Student Ministry
By Scotty Gibbons

Printed in the United States of America
ISBN: 1-880689-20-0
Copyright 2008, Scotty Gibbons and Onward Books, Inc.

Cover design by Scott Wiskus, Grand & Weller, grandandweller.com
Back cover photo by James Pauls, Eyecrave, eyecrave.com

Unless otherwise indicated, all Scripture references are from the *Holy Bible: New International Version*, copyright 1984, Zondervan Bible Publishers. Scripture quotations marked *The Message* are taken from *The Message: The New Testament, Psalms and Proverbs*, copyright 1993, 1994, 1995, NavPress Publishing Group.

dedication

To my wife, Casey, my best friend and the most beautiful person I know, inside and out. Let's grow old together!

contents

endorsements

The principles presented in *Carry-On* are being carried out in Scotty's life and ministry. This book is real life, not theory, which is why I encourage you to read it.

Monty Hipp
President, The C4 Group

The amazing journey of a high-impact youth pastor, *Carry-On* is a must-read for any youth leader who wants to grow and rediscover the joy of ministering to students.

Tom Elmore
Youth Pastor, Lakewood Church, Joel Osteen Ministries

Scotty enables youth pastors to define their vision and create the strategy to carry it out. He keeps the focus on "packing for the journey" based on relevance and effectiveness. *Carry-On* is a "must-read" for those committed to reaching this generation of youth.

Gary Beets
Missouri Fellowship of Christian Athletes

Carry-On is a practically powerful book that will both inspire and stir you as a leader in areas that are too often overlooked. More importantly, Scotty Gibbons is a voice to the generations of youth pastors and leaders who want to hear Jesus say, "well done."

Jeffery Portmann
Youth Director, Northwest Ministry Network

Engaging, enjoyable, and effective, Scotty hits a home run with *Carry-On*.

Josh McDowell
Best-Selling Author and Speaker

If I'm going to take the time to listen to someone's thoughts on ministry, they better have experience to match their ideas. Scotty is speaking from a roll-up-your-sleeves, I'm-not-leaving-youth-ministry, in-the-trenches-while-I'm-writing-this-book type of experience that works. If you're going to take the time to think about making it for the long haul without losing your passion, there's nobody better to download instructions from than Scotty Gibbons.

Nate Ruch
Executive Director, University Relations, North Central University
Co-Director, The Center for Youth and Leadership,
youthandleadership.com

Scotty Gibbons is a major voice in youth ministry today. Vocational or volunteer, any youth leader will find *Carry-On* to be a highly valuable resource.

Andy Braner
President, Kanakuk Colorado; Author, *Love This!, Duplicate This!*

I know a lot of youth pastors around the country and have to say that Scotty is, without a doubt, one of the best. I highly recommend this book for anyone serving in student ministry.

Kevin Moore
Youth Pastor, Oneighty®, Church On The Move

Carry-On is a much needed source for the youth leader. Being able to learn from Scotty Gibbons' vast experience as a youth leader will surely be a benefit and encouragement to anyone who takes on the venture of working with young people. Be sure to take *Carry-On* with you in your journey of youth ministry!

Kylan Booser
Host, 24/7 TV

Scotty has an amazing heart to help youth pastors and leaders by teaching them through the honest ups and downs of an incredible 15 years of youth ministry. There are few guys on the planet who are truly prepared, qualified, and committed to equipping people instead of simply building their own careers—Scotty is one of the few.

Jeff Deyo
Recording Artist, Founder of Pure Worship Institute

This book should be in every youth leader's library. It is like a getaway trip filled with godly guidance, experienced wisdom, and transparent reflection. Moreover, it seems to listen to me as much as it speaks to me. If you're like me, you always welcome another seasoned youth leader nearby. With Scotty's book, you'll have one at hand.

Jay Mooney
National Youth Director, Assemblies of God

acknowledgments

I've always felt like the acknowledgments section of a book is a bit cheesy, something like an acceptance speech at the Grammys. If there's anything that makes you look forward to a commercial break, that's it. In fact, I almost wished I could skip this part, sparing the reader the obligatory formality—that is, until I neared the end of this project. Reflecting back on this project, I realize that it would've been impossible if not for the tremendous help of so many.

So, at the risk of sounding cliché, I want to thank some incredible individuals.

First, to my parents for loving me, caring for me, encouraging me, and teaching me to set goals and accomplish dreams. More than anything, for always being there for me. I love you, Mom and Dad!

To my precious grandmother for your sweet prayers. Those prayers started before I was born and I still rely on them today. And to my grandfather for reading me Proverbs until I would fall asleep in your bed as a young boy.

To John Lindell, my pastor, my mentor, and my friend. Your character, commitment to the Word of God, and friendship mean more than I can possibly express. Thanks for everything!

To Hal Donaldson for the support and encouragement from the very beginning of this project. Your vote of confidence early on meant more than you realize. Thanks for being used of the Lord.

I want to especially say thanks to Scott Wiskus, my friend and the person most responsible for helping this book become a reality. I had a blast working with you on this adventure—even in the stressful times!

To Ken and Peggy Horn for your careful attention to detail and hands-on help with this fast-moving project.

To the Realife staff—Eric, Nathan, Adam, and Scott—you guys are gifts from God and I'm privileged to do student ministry together with you. Angie, thanks for fighting the daily battle of keeping my life sane, as best we can! Amy and Beth, thank you for your dedication and your hours of hard work. You make Realife happen.

To the volunteer leaders and students of Realife. Few things give me more personal satisfaction than encouraging and equipping the dedicated adult volunteers who work in our student ministry. Thanks for investing in students. The more I travel, the more convinced I am that my favorite group to speak to, go to camps with, and laugh and cry with are the students of Realife. You're the reason I'm so passionate about student ministry.

And finally, to my God, whom I adore and to whom I dedicate my life!

foreword

The Lord could not have sent me a more esteemed or effective youth pastor and friend. When I first met Scotty 16 years ago, my first impression was "This is a guy who loves God more than most." Over the years, that assessment has proved to be true. One of the great joys of my life has been to watch him develop as a youth pastor, a speaker and a leader of leaders.

With clear-headed simplicity, a passionate love for God and the delightful humor that has characterized his ministry, Scotty shares life-giving lessons for those who have been given the responsibility of ministering to students. *Carry-On* is not a call to copy Realife Student Ministries, and yet the principles contained in this book will encourage and inspire those who have set out on their own leadership journey.

As you read this book, my prayer is that in the midst of the busyness of life you will take time to pause and reflect on these principles. May their application in your life take you to the next level in your leadership and your passion for God.

John Lindell
Lead Pastor, James River Assembly

stories from my suitcase

"Food fight!"

To this day, I can still hear the war cry of the nearly 150 teenagers ringing in my ears. As hard as I've tried to forget, I still remember one particular aspect of Realife's first summer camp in vivid detail. At the time, I had been the youth pastor at James River Assembly for three years and student sign-ups for the event exceeded our expectations. Our camp was based out of a hotel about an hour away from the church, where we held morning and evening services in one of the meeting rooms. In the afternoons, we played games in a nearby field.

At the appointed hour on this particular afternoon, all of the students assembled on the field for what we called "the world's biggest food fight." Scattered across the field were trash cans filled with food—mashed potatoes, baked beans, applesauce, and the like. There were no rules. The whistle blew, and for 30 minutes, the students went crazy. Spaghetti was flying and pancake batter was smeared. To this day, it is one of the most enjoyable and disgusting things I have ever witnessed. As I stood there on the sidelines, I thought about ways to capture the experience so students wouldn't forget it—turns out that wouldn't be a problem.

As the reservoirs of edible ammunition ran dry, an unrecognizable junior high girl came up to me, her hair matted to her face with a surprisingly sticky combination of pancake batter and grape jelly. She asked where she could clean up, something I hadn't thought about. I looked around, noting that we had approximately 150 students completely covered in leftovers and precisely one hose with poor water pressure.

"Everybody, line up!" I yelled, realizing that we only had an hour before dinner was supposed to start.

As one of our volunteers began to hose the first girl down, the rest of the students lined up behind her,

each looking like the casualty of a Golden Corral buffet explosion.

"Pastor Scotty, this stuff isn't coming off!" the appointed hoser-offer worried aloud.

Apparently when food sits out in the sweltering heat for a few hours, it takes on an adhesive quality not unlike Super Glue.

After 15 minutes, only three of the 150 kids were recognizable and the students were getting visibly agitated under the hot summer sun. Not knowing what to do, I improvised, ordering the kids back to their hotel rooms to get cleaned up: "Dinner starts in 45 minutes! We'll go straight from dinner to the meeting room for service."

At dinner I picked up the vibe that students were less than thrilled with the outcome of the food fight. The mood was somber. I was getting angry eyes from some of the kindest students. It seemed like everyone was grumbling or complaining. One group of girls stood over the trash can, crying as they cut chunks of food out of their hair.

To add insult to injury, I was summoned to the front desk while I was eating. It turns out our students had used every last one of the hotel's available towels, and almost every one of them was ruined. Apparently, as our kids simultaneously hit the showers, the hotel ran out of hot water in a matter of minutes. With the evening service right around the corner, the students' only option was to wipe as much of the debris off as possible using the hotel's nice white towels. When the students used up all of the towels in their rooms, they went to the front desk to get more. This process repeated itself until the hotel was completely out of towels.

Outside the doors on our hallway, you could see piles of towels, stained every color of the rainbow, each concealing a plethora of formerly edible surprises. That would've been amusing except that I hadn't been planning on the $2,500 it cost the church to replace all of the hotel's towels, to say nothing about the damage caused to the hotel's plumbing, which apparently was not designed to withstand the mass absorption of foodstuffs.

In the service, the guest speaker had a difficult time connecting with the students. As he was up there struggling to preach, I watched girls literally pick chunks of food out of one another's hair. The guys were distracted too, clearing their arm- and leg-hair of dried pancake batter. It seemed like someone in every row was making a fun discovery—a bit of mashed potato in the ear canal or a piece of jelly-encrusted noodle in the nostril. I felt terrible for the speaker, who was thoroughly confused.

During the altar time, I was praying for a student when I was distracted by the unidentifiable wad of food sticking out of his ear.

To this day, former students talk about the "world's biggest food fight," and it's not because they had the world's best time. Chalk one up to inexperience!

Humble Beginnings

The food fight is one of several infamous occurrences in Realife history. To this day, one of my favorite things to do with my friends is sit around and rehash stories from the early days. Most of them make me laugh. Some of them make me want to cry. Many of them took place at one of our events. Early on, our events were, well, eventful. Typically, we would pick a theme, print tickets, and encourage our students to invite their friends to hear the gospel at a special service. At one point, the students were responding so well that we were holding one of these events every single week. To be honest, many of them run together in my mind, but this is my best attempt to recall one particular outreach.

We were holding our services in the church's fellowship hall, a medium-sized room that held about 100 kids. I wanted to paint a picture of what Christ went through on the cross near the end of my message, so I had some of our volunteers build a life-size cross out of old railroad timbers. The idea was to have the cross stand at the back of the stage throughout the event. At a certain point in my message, the lights would black out and I would climb on the cross. Highlighted by a single spotlight, I would finish my sermon from on high, eloquently articulating all that Christ endured on behalf of lost humanity.

It didn't work out like that. The first problem was that apparently we forgot to measure the room before building the larger-than-life cross. When we brought it into the room (minutes before the event, of course), it was too tall to stand up. With no time left to correct the oversight, we rested it against the wall at a 45 degree angle. While this variation on the vertical method added a certain dimension of geometric intrigue, it generally looked ridiculous.

The service started and we worked around the large crucifix that was now protruding out onto the stage. Halfway through my message, the lights went out. Allen, our lighting guy, missed his cue by a good five minutes, spoiling the climax.

"Not yet, Allen. You can turn the lights back on," I said, the audience snickering.

When the real blackout occurred, I climbed on the cross, and Allen activated our "spotlight," a medium-sized Maglite that was duct-taped to the bottom of the cross. That part went well, except with the lights out, I couldn't read my notes. Normally, I wouldn't have been that dependent on my notes, but I had been planning on reading a graphic description of the Crucifixion in medical terms. The rest of the room was pitch black and all eyes were focused on me, as I decided to ditch my notes. Here's somewhat of a replay:

"And do you know what Jesus did for you?" [Allen catches the cue on round two, the lights go out, and there's an awkward pause as I climb on the cross]

[flashlight turns on] "He …" [me fumbling with my notes] "He …

"He was crucified …" [more awkward silence as I decide to improvise]

"They nailed Him to a cross." [awkward silence] "With nails."

About that time I realized that I was preaching to the ceiling due to the slope of the cross. "And do you know what else they did to Him?," I asked the ceiling tiles, drawing a blank on the specific medical terminology.

I craned my neck forward to deliver my conclusion directly to the students: "It was so bad … I can't even describe it."

By the grace of God, students were saved. But I can assure you, I had nothing to do with it.

Live and Learn

In many ways, these stories are typical examples of my leadership early on. I loved God, I loved teenagers, and I wanted to make a difference. I had plenty of vision, but it often seemed to get lost in translation.

Everything seemed perfect in my head, but it rarely worked out that way in reality.

To some extent, we're all in over our heads in student ministry. We want students to encounter Christ and be changed. That's the relatively easy part. The hard part is figuring out how to facilitate that as a leader, whether you're leading a group of seven or 700.

When I came on staff in 1993, James River was a young church that had just moved into its first building. Although the church had a Sunday morning attendance of 600, there was no youth ministry.

When Pastor John Lindell offered me a part-time job working with the youth, I initially declined the offer, feeling inadequate to the task. I enjoyed volunteering at the church, but was also balancing a full-time college schedule and another job. After a few more conversations, though, I sensed God's leading and agreed to become the church's part-time youth pastor.

In those days, my entire approach to leadership in student ministry could be summed up as "live and learn." I was learning all kinds of lessons, because I was making all kinds of mistakes. I still make mistakes, of course, but fortunately they usually don't require closing down a hotel. If you would have told me then that one day I would be youth pastor to more than 1,000 students, I wouldn't have believed you. It never entered my mind that one day James River would be a congregation 10,000 strong, one of the country's fastest growing churches.

A lot has changed since 1993. Today, we reach a lot more students and we have a lot more help. I'm privileged to have the support of an incredible staff and more than 200 volunteer leaders. As I think about all the incredible things that happen daily at Realife, I can't help but smile about how this journey began.

My office was a partial cubicle in the classroom where we met for youth service, which at the time was attended by a grand total of 12 students (on a good night).

As I sat at my desk that first day, it dawned on me that I didn't know what I was supposed to be doing. I wondered, *What do youth pastors do anyway?* Unsure of the answer, arranging the supplies on my desk seemed like a good place to start. After about 30 minutes, I realized that there are only so many ways one can arrange a stapler, a notebook, and a cup filled with pens. Having exhausted my options, I sat there thinking, *Now what?*

As I stared at the wall, it occurred to me that I should prepare something for our first youth group meeting—turns out that was a great idea since the service was only a couple of hours away. Before I knew it (or had a chance to prepare much of anything), "they" started to show up.

I swallowed hard and took the six steps from my "office" to the front of the classroom to greet them as they arrived. All 12 students showed up for my first night, each taking a seat in the single row I had diligently set up at the front of the classroom. At seven o'clock, I decided it was safe to leave my post as the greeter to start the service. The kids stopped talking and we just looked at one another for a moment, the fluorescent lights humming above our heads.

Our church always started its services with worship, so opening with a song seemed like the natural thing to do.

"Let's stand and worship?" I more asked than told the students.

The students looked around and one by one stood to their feet as I began clapping on beat. Once everyone was standing, I began singing (without accompaniment): "This is the day ... This is the day ... That the Lord has made ... That the Lord has ma–"

I opened one of my eyes to a worship leader's worst nightmare—everyone staring forward blankly. *Awkward.* I think one kid was blowing a bubble with his gum while a couple of others whispered at the end of the row. One thing's for sure: no one was singing the echo part.

"All righty! That's enough for worship," I conceded. As you might imagine, the rest of the service was less than stellar.

Well Done

I hope the stories I've shared from my journey in student ministry demonstrate that you are not alone. It's good to know that you don't have to be a perfect leader. You don't have to have all of the answers. My experience has confirmed what the Scripture teaches—God's strength is made perfect in our weakness (1 Corinthians 1:26-28; 2 Corinthians 12:9). Having come a long way since those early examples, I think the most important thing I could tell you about leadership is that it's a journey.

As a leader, you have an ultimate destination, accomplishing God's will for your life (Matthew 7:21-23; 1 John 2:17).

Your ultimate goal is to please Him with your life and in your leadership.

When you stand before God one day, and your work is tested with fire, you don't want it to be burned up (1 Corinthians 3:10-15). Your ultimate destination is that place where you hear Jesus say, "Well done" (Matthew 25:14-30). It would be great if we could all arrive at our ultimate destination today, but the reality is that you're still here on earth because God has something for you to do.

There are a lot of stops along the way to your ultimate destination, significant milestones on your journey. Perhaps you'll get married or, if you're married, you'll have kids. You'll reach that one student who's away from God. You'll start that small group program. You'll break that attendance barrier. You'll graduate that first class of students from discipleship or you'll lead that first missions trip. Milestones give you the opportunity to stop and appreciate what's been accomplished, anticipating what lies ahead. But you don't park at a milestone. You pause long enough to take in the surroundings and celebrate them, and then you move on. You never stop permanently because you're on a journey, most of which will be spent in transit—traveling the long road from one milestone to the next on your way to your ultimate destination.

You probably realize by now that the majority of your leadership journey isn't characterized by the excitement of the big event. Instead, it's the day-in, day-out details that lead up to the event and follow after it. It's working and often not seeing the results. It's administrating. It's phone calls and emails. It's long days and lots of meetings. It's driving that kid home from small group. It's writing a letter of apology to the hotel your students nearly destroyed. I don't share this to discourage you, because the journey is well worth it.

The reality, though, is that many youth leaders find themselves in a place where they wonder if the journey is worth it—worth the trouble, worth the discouragement, worth the heartache. I'm being candid because I want you to have realistic expectations. I want you to make it over the long haul in student ministry and find joy in your journey.

For some, joy is the furthest thing from your mind when you think about your student ministry. There was a day when you were passionate about students, when you believed that what you did mattered in this life and for eternity. There was a time when your responsibilities weren't just part of the job, tasks to be completed. Every single week I get phone calls and emails from youth pastors who are ready to give up. They've all but thrown in the towel. Ready to resign, they're simply looking for the right opportunity to raise the white flag. They don't feel the love and support of their pastor. They don't know how much more criticism they can take. Mounting conflicts keep them awake at night. They're overwhelmed with their schedule and their responsibilities. They're working to the point of burnout, but they don't see results.

The more opportunities I have to speak with youth leaders, the less surprised I am that their average length of service is between eight months and a year. And at the same time, I'm increasingly convinced it doesn't have to be that way. If, as you read this book, you find yourself discouraged, I want to remind you of something you probably know deep down. Your ultimate goal in student ministry isn't to reach some numerical goal, or to build a program, or to please everyone in your congregation. You're not in student ministry for the accolades or the affirmation, you're responding to the call of God. An amazing thing I've noticed over the years is that as a result of your obedience, the situations that are your biggest challenges will eventually become some of your biggest victories— if you don't give up.

Maybe you feel like I did early on, clueless and completely unprepared. That's OK. God doesn't need your wisdom or power. Take a moment to stop and think about that. God isn't looking for a youth leader with all of the answers. He doesn't need your preaching or your programs.

He's looking for a leader who recognizes their own inadequacy, yet still has a desire to do something that will count for eternity.

He wants to take you on a journey.

After 15 years in student ministry, my encouragement to you is simple: carry on. Stick with it. As my friend Monty Hipp often says at the end of a conversation, "Stay in the journey." You and I are on different journeys, but I'm thankful we'll be sharing the next few miles together. As we do, it's my prayer that you are encouraged and equipped to be more effective in student ministry than you ever imagined possible. Carry on.

packing potential

It seems like my suitcase is always the last one to surface. It doesn't matter what airport I'm in, where I'm going, or where I've been. The siren sounds and a hundred other bags proudly parade past, each a little worse for the wear. Eager owners crowd around the carousel, plucking their bags from the conveyor belt as a child would pick a puppy from the rest of the litter. I stand back—one eye on my Blackberry, the other on the bags—waiting to reunite my carry-on and my checked luggage.

Sometimes while I wait for my suitcase, I watch fellow travelers pick up their bags, guessing which one belongs to whom. The overstuffed canvas duffel with what appears to be a large sweat stain? It probably belongs to the rather large gentleman who had me pinned in my window seat from Cincinnati to Springfield. I'm guessing the leopard suitcase set belongs to the middle-aged woman wearing the leopard jacket and shoes. And if I were a betting man, I'd say James Bond's gunmetal gray briefcase belongs to the guy who wore his Bluetooth earpiece through the entire flight (even though phone calls aren't allowed at 30,000 feet).

The Secret

You can tell a lot about a person by the kind of luggage they carry. Many people go for function; they don't care what their bag looks like. Others carry designer luggage that makes some sort of statement (usually, the statement is "I spent way too much money on these bags"). A privileged few have bags with all of the latest features—compartments, pockets, zippers, attachments, and gadgets. Personally, I don't care whether or not my suitcase is "cool." I care that it works. I'm not interested in making a fashion statement as I walk from one gate to the next in between flights.

As interesting as it sounds, I don't need my suitcase to double as a table or a wheelchair or a flotation device.

I'm interested in arriving at my destination with all of my belongings intact and accessible.

My suitcase was given to me several years ago, a Christmas gift from my parents. It's one of those gifts that keeps on giving, serving me well trip after trip. It's not fancy or much to look at; it doesn't have an expandable compartment or a built-in compass. Tried and true, it gets the job done. It's simple, it's sturdy, and it protects my belongings from the various "acts of God" that only enter the equation when an airline is involved.

All of this talk about my suitcase causes me to wonder where in the world (literally) it could be. The number of bags emerging from the mysterious hole in the wall is waning. The light is no longer flashing, and though I'm not sure, I think I've seen some grandma's floral-pattern suitcase circle at least 50 times. Giving up, I decide to go to the baggage claim office, when someone yells my name.

"Pastor Scotty!"

"Hello there," I smile to a 20-something guy who looks vaguely familiar.

"Hey, my name is Kyle and I've gone to James River Assembly for a few years now. I'm about to graduate from college and I'm going to be a youth pastor ..."

"That's cool," I interrupt.

"Yeah, I've gone to Realife a few times, but I didn't really have time to get involved. But, I was wondering if I could ask you a question?"

"Sure," I reply, glancing over his shoulder to see a grandmotherly figure struggling to get her floral-print suitcase to dismount the conveyor belt.

"I'm wondering what the secret has been to Realife's numerical and spiritual growth over the years. What's the key?"

I briefly glance again over Kyle's shoulder. Grandma is now officially fighting with her suitcase and I wonder what might happen if she loses. I imagine her refusing to let go, even as it pulls her through the hole in the wall into the unexplored bowels of the Springfield airport. I want to laugh, but I don't want Kyle to think I'm laughing at his question.

The Truth

Fortunately, it's a question I'm well acquainted with. As I have the opportunity to interact with youth leaders around the country, I'm often asked about Realife. Specifically, youth pastors want to know "the secret." They want their student ministry to break some attendance barrier. They want the teenagers in their group to "get it" spiritually.

After 15 years in student ministry at a thriving church and after traveling the country many times over speaking to young people and their leaders, I've come to the conclusion that there is no secret (whether you're talking about Realife or any other student ministry).

As convenient as it would be, there isn't a Miracle Grow of the youth group variety.

There is no silver bullet. It's not that small groups have been the key to Realife's growth. Or, that one day we had an epiphany about our approach to the youth service and, from that point on, we've experienced explosive growth. It's not our events or the preaching. There is no secret sauce. And while there isn't a quick-fix, there is something you can and should do if you're going to experience success in student ministry (in fact, it's what this book is about).

The fact that there is no secret does not mean there isn't a reason. In other words, there may not be a one-size-fits-all solution for growing your ministry, but there's still a cause when things do grow. Ultimately, what's happened at Realife can only be attributed to God's sovereign work. The first time I visited James River, there was a sense that something unique was happening, but we had no idea God would do all that He has. We certainly didn't have any aces up our sleeve. God gets all of the credit and all of the glory.

As a leader, I'm interested in results, not secrets. One of the advantages of being around awhile in student ministry is that you see trends come and go. If you pay attention to the fact that fads are here one day and gone the next, you'll develop an appreciation for the elements that are foundational to any healthy ministry. When youth leaders are looking for the fad or the fix, they usually don't want to hear Sunday School answers like "prayer" and "the Bible." Often, they assume those things cognitively, but overlook them in practice. And yet, the plain things are the main things.

As a ministry, we bathe everything in prayer. Time and again we see God move in powerful ways and I am absolutely convinced it's because we acknowledge that our best efforts will fail every time if we don't have God's help. That's why we prioritize our weekly prayer meetings, using those opportunities to seek the Lord and teach students about the power of prayer. Another simple thing that makes all the difference is an overarching emphasis on God's Word. Because I'm interested in results, I preach the whole counsel of God's Word to our students and teach our volunteers to process their life and leadership in light of the Scriptures. After all, it's not my abilities as an orator that change lives and it's not Realife's programs—it's the power of God's enduring Word.

Much more will be said about the power of prayer and of the Scriptures for success in student ministry. I would strongly encourage you as a leader not to skip past the previous paragraph like it's some obligatory spiritual caveat we need to get out of the way before moving on to the "practical stuff." As you'll see in this book, your student ministry suitcase isn't some bag of tricks.

There are no substitutes for the presence of God working in and through your ministry, so keep the plain things the main things.

To me, one of the remarkable things about God's spiritual work is that He chooses to carry it out through His people. As Christians, we are partners with God, co-laborers with Christ (1 Corinthians 3:9). If I had to give an earthly explanation for how God is working at James River or at Realife, I would say it's through leadership. The phrase "Everything rises and falls on leadership" has quickly become a cliché in many organizations, but that doesn't make it any less true. You can give a great leader a terrible situation, and they'll rise above it. They'll make turning things around look easy. The opposite is also true. You could give a poor leader the ideal scenario, serving it up on a silver platter. Even with everything going for them, they'd still manage to lead the thing right into the ground.

Over the years at Realife, programs have come and gone, so have structures, themes, and methods. All of these things have their appropriate place in ministry, but their place is secondary to leadership. They are simply resources in a leader's hand. Good leaders will use the resources at their disposal to take people where they could never go on their own.

What's true about Realife is true about your student ministry. Think about the areas of your ministry that are thriving. Behind that growth there's probably a good leader. If you're having a problem in an area and you want to get to the root of it, look to the leader of that ministry.

Good or bad, leadership makes all of the earthly difference in your student ministry. Your leadership has an impact on the growth of your group, spiritually and numerically. Your leadership affects the type of volunteer leaders you attract and it affects how they in turn lead your students and your programs. It will make the difference between an apathetic bunch of students who are cynical toward Christ and His Church and a group of teenagers who are in love with God, committed to carrying out His cause in a lost world.

Fanny Pack

As Kyle and I stand in the baggage claim, I start to laugh—partly because out of the corner of my eye, I'm seeing someone's grandma showing her bag who's boss, and partly because the notion that there's some secret to success in student ministry is laughable in and of itself.

Kyle and I start walking toward the baggage claim office as I answer his question. "Leadership is a journey. If you're going to be successful over the long haul in student ministry, and if you're going to enjoy the journey, you've got to pack well for the trip," I say as I point at his shiny, somewhat-new suitcase.

"When you don't pack well for a trip, it's hard to enjoy yourself, much less be effective. When you pack well, there's no limit to the adventure you might have."

I explain to Kyle that when I started, my student ministry suitcase was nearly empty.

I only had a few items; fortunately, they were some of the most important—a love for God, a heart for teenagers, and faith that

God wanted to use my life for His purpose. Honestly, I didn't even need a suitcase at that point, a fanny pack would've held my student ministry knowledge and experience.

I've mentioned that I made mistakes in student ministry early and often. We all do. The important thing is to make a point of learning from your mistakes. Almost every lesson I've learned on my journey is somewhere in my suitcase. You can ask anyone on my staff. One of the fun things about leading a staff is trying to teach them the things you had to learn the hard way. It's easier said than done because most people have to learn things on their own. At different times I'll ask all kinds of questions of my staff, about this upcoming event or about that parent situation or about an important meeting. From time to time, I can tell that the team is ready to move on to the next order of business, but I'll want to talk a little more about the rental of the vans or the guest speaker's arrangements or my expectations for the service. My goal isn't to micromanage or waste anyone's time. In those moments I'm pulling lessons out of my suitcase.

Fortunately, my student ministry suitcase isn't just full of past mistakes. Back in the day, when I was still fanny-packin' it, I realized there were a lot of people out there whom I could learn from. I surrounded myself with leaders I respected, read every relevant book I could get my hands on, observed what others did well, and observed what others did poorly. Gradually, my suitcase started to fill up. I found that the longer and farther I traveled, the easier things became.

Today, I'm traveling to places on my leadership journey that I've never been before, and while I can't anticipate everything I'm going to encounter along the way, I know I'm prepared. My carry-on is packed. Early on in my journey I made it a goal not just to survive my years in student ministry or to be successful in them, but to continue packing my bags for whatever the future may hold.

450-Foot Flotation Device

When I think about packing, I think about Noah. You know the story. God gets fed up with the wickedness of humanity and decides to wipe the floor with every living creature. In His mercy, though, God chooses to spare one righteous man and his family. That man, of course, is Noah.

Noah was a pretty cool guy. Not only was he blameless, but he also walked with God at a time when few people did. The New Testament refers to him as a "preacher of righteousness." The thing that really impresses me, though, about Noah, is his incredible obedience when God asks him to build an enormous boat and then pack it with two of every living creature. Have you ever really stopped to think about that? It's not like Noah could just hoof it down to Home Depot and open a line of credit. Could you imagine that exchange?

"You guys have 12 months same as cash, right?"

"Sure do. No money down and no payments until 3010 BC," the clerk replies, not aware of the fact that Home Depot wouldn't be around to collect payment in 3010 BC.

Smirking, Noah replies under his breath, "That won't be a problem; sign me up!'"

"Great! What can we get you?"

"Well, I'm going to need a fourth of the cedars of Lebanon, a power saw, a hammer, about 500,000 nails, and this box of Snickers. Have everything delivered to 1 Righteous Way in Chaldea—except for the candy bars; I'll take those now."

I don't think building the ark was quite that easy. This wasn't something Noah learned in shop class, nor was it a DIY project for the average weekend warrior. On top of that, he had the added pressure of building a seaworthy vessel capable of carrying his family and most of animalia (the aquatic creatures and dinosaurs notwithstanding). Once Noah managed to finish building the ark, he was faced with the delicate task of packing it.

Certainly, God was involved in the whole process. Did He miraculously direct the animals into their individual compartments and cages? Maybe God brought all baby animals on board the ark to save space and to keep the load light. Or maybe Noah was an experienced traveler and had some tricks of his own—you know, rolling the snakes, hanging the bats, stacking the rodents, storing the kangaroos' food in their pouches. I'm not completely sure, but I wonder if the game Barrel of Monkeys is named for one of Noah's packing techniques.

Packing the ark would be difficult. You could only afford to bring the essentials, lest the boat sink. Then again, you couldn't just leave one of the African elephants behind to lighten the load, spelling the end of a species (not to mention risking a PETA lawsuit). As you brought all of the animals on board, you'd have to arrange them carefully. I know that the lion will lie down with the lamb in heaven, but putting their cages next to one another on the Good Ship Salvation probably wouldn't be good. And this is important, because if the lion ate the lamb, the Jews might have been sacrificing penguins in Jesus' day.

Smooth Sailing

Before he ever set sail, Noah packed his bags and his boat. His obedience wasn't easy. In fact, it was a lot of hard work and sacrifice. But you can be sure that when it started to rain, Noah was glad he had listened to God. Effective packing makes for smooth sailing. As much fun as we've had with Noah, there are a couple of important lessons we can learn from his experience packing the ark.

1. Your Potential Depends on Your Packing

First, your potential as a leader—where you go and what you accomplish—depends largely on how you pack. Your journey will be directly impacted, positively or negatively, by either your preparation or your lack thereof. When I'm talking about packing, I'm not talking about having it all together; if you read the last chapter, you know that I don't claim to have it all figured out.

The person who packs their bag is admitting they don't have it all together, they don't have the resources they need to be effective in and of themselves.

God is looking for leaders who have packed their bags in faith, even if they don't know where they're going. Think about the men and women God used in the Bible. He didn't choose perfect leaders (Jesus being the exception, of course), or people who had every detail mapped out. He chose people who positioned themselves to be used, packing their bags for whatever journey God might take them on.

You have incredible potential in Christ. God's plan for you is greater than you could ever hope to imagine.

The extent to which you realize His plan is directly correlated with your willingness to prepare for it.

2. Your Packing Affects Others

Second, God saved Noah through his act of faith, but Noah wasn't the only one impacted by it. Noah's entire family was saved because of his leadership. The human race was preserved. Ultimately, we're here on planet Earth today because Noah obeyed God, building and packing the ark.

As a leader, your choices have a trickle-down effect. Your decision to pack will result in positive change in the lives of people you may never meet. I hope that you're not in student ministry because you think it's cool or because you want to build a crowd or exert your influence. All of those things are secondary at best. One day the "ark" that is your student ministry is going to be history. What will matter then are the lives that will be changed because of it.

You may think, *Well, I only have 30 students in my group.* Be careful about looking at your group through earthly eyes. Even if you move past the fact that each of those 30 students have their own spheres of influence that you impact indirectly, you still don't know what God might do with just one of your students. So, you're not youth pastor to thousands. One of your students might be one day. You may never travel outside of the United States, but one of your students might grow up to be an incredible missionary who lays down his or her life that entire tribes might be saved.

That kid picking his nose on the back row may one day write the spiritual songs of a generation.

The awkward girl who always lingers hours after the service has concluded may write books that change lives, or may raise a child who will. The only way you'll find out is by packing your bags today.

Plain Black Pack

As we approach the baggage claim office, I see my suitcase sitting just inside the door. For some reason, it never made it onto the conveyor belt. Whatever happened, I'm glad to see it. Kyle and I continue to talk as we walk toward the parking lot. He has his shiny new suitcase and I have my plain black pack. We are both on a journey.

As you read this book, know that there's an incredible journey ahead of you as a leader in student ministry. God wants to do more in and through you than you could imagine. I know that could sound cheesy or cliché, but it's true. Think about that for a moment. Do you really believe it? The question isn't whether or not God is willing to take you on a remarkable journey. The question is whether or not you'll prepare for that journey. If you're looking for the secret sauce, the silver bullet, or the quick fix, I'm sorry to inform you there is no such thing. This book isn't about building your program, hitting some numerical goal, or even reaching that student God has placed on your heart. It's about you reaching your ultimate destination and making the most of the milestones along the way. And if that's going to happen, you've got to pack. So grab your suitcase and let's get started.

tagging your luggage

You're excited to go on a journey and you're eager to start packing. Before you start throwing things into your student ministry suitcase, there's one thing you need to do. It's so foundational, you may not have even thought about it. Tagging your luggage is an important first step on your journey. In fact, there are three tags you want on your bag that make for a successful trip. You can pack everything else, but if you don't mark your luggage, you're likely to lose it.

Not Your Average Bag Tag

The first luggage tag gives you the opportunity to get creative and have some fun. You need to find something that will easily catch your eye, distinguishing your bag from everyone else's, and then figure out a way to attach it to your bag. It could be anything. For a while, my bag blended in with everyone else's, that is, until my wife got hold of it. Now, my simple black suitcase has an '80s neon-green gripper covering the handle. Initially, I wasn't exactly thrilled about the idea. It's kind of like a Christian can-koozie for my suitcase; the graphics printed on it remind me that angels are watching over me (and apparently the contents of my suitcase, thank goodness).

Initially, I was a bit embarrassed by the addition of the gripper, but I do have to admit, my bag is easy to spot at the baggage claim because it is uniquely tagged. You could use anything that's both noticeable and durable. Some tie a ribbon to their bag or mark it with colored duct tape or a gaudy keychain. Not only is my bag easy to spot, but thanks to my little green friend, the chance that someone else is going to confuse it for their own is greatly reduced. If a confused traveler still managed to pick up my bag, they'd put it right back the moment they saw the pixelated angel Gabriel staring up at them, promising heavenly retribution for their trespass, albeit accidental.

At its core, spiritual leadership is about standing out from the crowd.

There's something about good leaders that attracts the attention of everyone around them.

It's not that they have to be the loudest or the life of the party; something about their presence demands attention. They love God wholeheartedly and they don't care what people think. They aren't interested in playing games; they're interested in getting things done.

Unfortunately, many youth workers spend their energy trying to blend in with the teenagers, rather than standing out as their leader. Instead of focusing their efforts on reaching students, they're content to look the part. Maybe you've seen the 35-year-old youth pastor who's still trying to squeeze into the size 30 jeans he wore in high school. All of his T-shirts are from Hollister and he wouldn't be caught dead without one of those really wide leather wristbands that looks like it belonged to a Roman centurion. For a brief minute you think he might be a teenager, with his fake-bake tan, platinum-tipped follicles, and use of "hip" phrases like "da bomb." But then you see him loading his normal-looking family in the minivan, and you realize it's a mirage. He's not a teenager after all.

This may surprise you, but students aren't looking for someone who's just like them. They're looking for a leader who stands out. They want to follow someone they can look up to, even if they don't shop at Hollister. They're looking for authenticity. They're looking for a genuine love for God. They're looking for someone who will love and accept them. They're not looking for a fashion statement; they can get that at school.

I'm not implying that relating to students on their level isn't important; it is important but it's secondary. I'm not suggesting that you show up to preach in the clothes you wear at your corporate day job, but students would rather follow someone who stands out from the crowd because of who they are as a leader, than follow a shallow leader who spends his prep time for the service in front of the bathroom mirror rather than on his knees.

My point is that, ultimately, students will respect you as their leader because of who you are and what you stand for, not because you're wearing a brand of clothing they like. Great if they happen to like your shirt, but your preppy polo isn't going to convince a young person to follow you. If that's why they're following you, be sure to keep up with the latest trends, or you're going to lose them as soon as vintage T-shirts come back in style.

If you're going to stand out from the crowd, let it be because you're a spiritual leader.

You'll stand out if you approach life and leadership with two simple, but powerful, perspectives. First, approach God relationally rather than religiously. We'll talk about this more later on, but don't hurry past this point just because it's simple. Many young people, particularly those raised in Christian homes, have a religious understanding of God, but they don't own it relationally. When students listen to your sermons, do they hear about a God you've read about or a God you walk with? Model an authentic and passionate pursuit of Christ for the students in your group, one that affects every aspect of your life, from your attitude in adversity to the shows you choose to watch on TV. Don't be content to go through the motions or to play some religious game, because when you do, you blend in with the crowd.

Second, as a leader, you should approach life with an eternal perspective rather than an earthly one. As a leader, do you ever stop and think about the fact that one day you'll stand before God? When your life on this earth comes to a close, you'll give Him an account for your life and leadership. In that moment, God's not going to overlook a lack of spiritual leadership because He enjoyed the ice breakers you used to open your services. The angels aren't going to be impressed with your ability to draw a crowd. The saints in the great cloud of witnesses aren't going to ask if you have any leftover event T-shirts. What will matter is that you faithfully carried out your assignment, that you led students to Jesus. When you view your leadership through an eternal perspective, everything changes. You have an opportunity to make an eternal difference with your earthly actions, so stand out from the crowd.

Because I want to lead from an eternal perspective, I try to approach each ministry opportunity as if it were my last. When you do that, there aren't "big events" and "normal services." Every opportunity is significant. That's why I give my best in study, I pour my heart out in prayer, and I get up and preach with passion. When I'm done, I'm exhausted because I made a decision to "leave it all on the field," as my football coach used to say. And yet, as tired as I might be from an earthly vantage point, I know I've completed my eternal assignment.

Name Tag

The second bag tag you're going to need is for your name. This may be the most important of the tags because it identifies who you are.

I was traveling with a friend recently on a ministry trip. While we were waiting to board the plane, I was catching up on some emails in the gate area. I didn't get very far before hearing a familiar name being paged over the intercom: "Bruce Gibbons, please come to the desk at gate C6." A little side note: my first name is actually Bruce, Scott is my middle name and I've gone by Scotty my whole life. It turns out the gate agent recognized me from church, and he knew me only as Scotty. Basically, he called me to the gate to ask if my name really was Bruce. When I told him it was, he laughed at me in disbelief, looking left and then right to confirm that he was the only one entrusted with such sensitive information.

That was really awkward, I thought as I sat back down.

As insignificant as your name might seem, it's actually very important. Your name represents you—it's the tag on the outside that represents your character on the inside, who you are and what you're about. It's not enough that you stand out from the crowd attracting the attention of those around you. Once you've attracted their attention, they're going to start checking you out. They want to know who you really are.

In the Bible, names are significant, particularly in the Old Testament. A name carries a reputation; it's synonymous with one's character. The Bible says that a good name is to be desired (Proverbs 22:1). I believe that's because when someone hears your name, certain thoughts come to their mind. For example, you think of one thing when you hear the name Billy Graham, and you think of something entirely different when you hear the name Adolf Hitler.

What do the students in your group think about when they hear your name? Are you the life of the party? The spiritual drill sergeant? The busy bee? Or do you model a love for God and His people? Do the students in your ministry know your character? Would they trust you with the truth about their situation? When they think of you, do they envision a spiritual leader? Are you known as someone who walks and talks with God? Can they count on the fact that you base your decisions on biblical principles?

This is incredibly important in student ministry. In any leadership situation, who you are is reproduced in your followers. Junior and senior high students are especially impressionable. As teenagers, students are beginning to form their own worldview and convictions. They are establishing habits, good or bad. It's wonderful if you attend their basketball games and piano recitals, great if you're there for them in the hour of crisis. You should be; your presence in these settings opens up an opportunity for influence. The question is, in those moments, will it make a difference in the right direction?

Your first responsibility to your students is to be their spiritual leader, not to build a program or run a service. When your students see the name tag on your luggage, they see who you are.

Destination Tag

The third and final tag for your luggage is the destination tag. You know what I'm talking about—that sticky tag the airline attendant puts on your bag, routing it to its next destination.

When you stand out from the crowd and are known for your character, people will want to follow you.

Where will you lead them? By taking a quick look at your luggage, the people around you should know where you're going. I'm not talking about your ultimate destination. That's a given. I'm talking about where you're taking your students on the next few legs of the journey.

Recently, when I showed up at the airport to catch a flight, I was assisted by a gentleman who was almost certainly convinced that he was God's gift to the airlines. And since Delta apparently doesn't make a lapel pin for gate agents who arrive at such an elite status, this man (whom we'll call "Bill") employed a variety of other techniques to assure me that I was in good hands.

Bill typed fast—really fast—so fast that you almost wondered if he were really typing or just crunching the keyboard like a toddler at a piano. He spoke down to me, as if it were my first time on the "big metal bird," and he did so loudly. It felt like everyone in line behind me was at the counter with me. And then there were the simultaneous mutterings. Randomly, Bill would interrupt his own diatribes to mutter something to himself or to a co-worker in another language. And we're not just talking Spanish here. Bill went out of his way to let me know that he was multi-lingual.

Anyway, just when I thought checking in couldn't take any longer or be any more humiliating, Bill holds up two destination tags—fresh off the printer—one on either side of his head. He spoke especially loud, as if the information was especially important:

"These are your destination tags. Your bags are checked through to Seattle. Can you verify?"

"Verify what?" I asked, unfamiliar with Bill's procedure.

"That your bags are supposed to go to Seattle!" Bill raised his voice.

"Yes, I'm going to Seattle, and I'd like my bags to go with me," I explained in an intentionally hushed tone.

"That's why I need you to verify! You don't want these bags … *dieser Kerl ist wirklich langsam* … to end up in Houston!" Bill retorted, pausing for dramatic effect. "Mistakes happen."

Bill was a bit dramatic, but he understood the importance of destination. It should go without saying, but before you can lead someone somewhere, you've got to know where you're going and how to get there. Proverbs 29:18 (*The Message*) says that "If people can't see what God is doing, they stumble all over themselves; but when they attend to what He reveals, they are most blessed." Can the people around you see what God is doing in your ministry? Do they understand where you're going? If they know where you're going, do they see how all of the different elements of your ministry are working together to take you there?

Your responsibility as a leader is to develop a vision for your student ministry, make sure it's in alignment with the vision of your pastor, and then steward the ministry's various resources toward that end.

What is your God-given vision for your student ministry? What are the next few milestones on your journey?

What is God wanting to do in your student ministry? In your church? In your community? In our world? How is He wanting you to be a part of that? How can you best utilize the resources He's entrusted to you to bring that vision to pass?

Unfortunately, a lot of youth leaders never define their vision or their strategy for accomplishing that vision. Instead, they're content to plan services and activities because that's what the church has always done. Or worse yet, they reduce student ministry to an entertaining teenage babysitting service, an alternative to sitting at home playing video games. It might be helpful to ask yourself some practical questions as a leader. Why do you have a youth service? What is the goal of your small group ministry? What is the best way to utilize your volunteer leaders if you're going to accomplish your vision?

Your plan doesn't have to be perfect. There's no way you could know all of the steps you're going to take along your way. The important thing is that you're leading your students in the right direction. God will direct you as you listen intently to Him on the journey. At Realife, we have God's vision for our student ministry. It's in alignment with what God is doing in our church as a whole (and by the way, that's important). As a matter of fact, we've adopted James River's process for carrying out that vision: "Love, Live, Lead."

First, we want students to experience God's love in a way that transforms them from the inside out. Next, we want that love to change the way they live. Finally, we want them to take that change to others by leading them to God's love. Everything we do at Realife falls strategically within one of those categories, from our services to our small groups to our missions trips. If something doesn't fit under love, live, or lead, we don't do it. We've changed our strategy before and we'll probably update it in the future; the important thing is to be sensitive to God's leadership in carrying out His vision.

Once you have God's vision, it's important that you communicate it. Vision casting is a powerful force that is critical if you're going to go anywhere in leadership.

As a leader, you go ahead of the group and see things they may not see.

Then, you help them see what you see. People need to know where you're going. Otherwise, you can't blame them for not following.

I learned a lot about vision as a young youth pastor. A leader should cast vision both individually and corporately. When our group was a lot smaller, we had a handful of students who thought they were too cool to worship God. When it came time to worship, their apathy would affect the spiritual temperature of the entire group. One of the students' names was Carter. He wanted to do the right thing, but cared too much about what his friends thought of him.

As I gave Carter a ride home one night after service, I began to talk with him about vision. I told him what I saw: a group of teenagers who were missing out on all that God had for them because no one would lead them. I challenged him to envision what could happen if he would be a leader in worship. The next time I saw him, I painted the picture again and encouraged him to stand for God. At our next youth service, before worship began, I encouraged Carter to focus on God and forget about his friends.

I watched Carter that night during worship. Nervously at first, he began to sing along with the worship leader. When we hit the chorus, he raised one of his hands halfway and closed his eyes to focus on God. I was so proud of him. By the end of the worship set, all of his friends had followed his cue and begun to focus on the Lord. It wasn't long before those students were some of our most committed worshipers. Instead of bringing the group down in worship, they raised the spiritual temperature. Why? Because Carter got hold of vision.

A lack of vision can make a difference in the other direction, too. I hadn't been a youth pastor very long when I was invited to dinner at the house of one of our volunteer leaders. When I arrived, I was surprised to see that nearly the entire volunteer leadership team was there. As dinner began, it was clear that their main goal wasn't to get to know me better. They had an agenda. One by one, they went around the table and told me the things I needed to change about the student ministry. If that doesn't make you say, "Pass the potatoes," I don't know what will! Part of the problem with these leaders was that they were taking the wrong approach, and part of the problem was that I had failed to cast vision for the team, explaining what we were doing and why we were doing it. In the midst of the vision vacuum, the leaders got restless and tried taking matters into their own hands.

What You See Is What You Get

As a leader, you'll find that you're continually casting vision. It's not just something you do once a year or when you introduce big changes.

Every single week I'm casting vision in one way or another, whether it's speaking privately with an individual on my staff or publicly with a group of new leaders. From time to time, we all need to be reminded where we're going, how we're going to get there, and why it matters. Your role as a leader is to know when your team needs vision and how it should be communicated.

There are a few simple, but important steps I recommend when casting vision. I've found that the art of communicating possibility has as much to do with the order in which you move through these steps, as it does with the steps themselves.

1. Listen to God

First and most important, is discerning God's vision for your situation. I would suggest praying specifically about where your group is now and where God wants to take it in the future. I rarely walk away from my prayer time with a seven-step plan for doing the Lord's work; maybe you can relate. Instead, I get a raw sense, impression, or direction in my heart.

2. Work Out the Details

Once you know where you're supposed to go in general terms, take some time to prayerfully process what realizing that vision might look like in your specific situation. Write down ways you could lead your group to that destination. Decide what things will need to change in order and how they need to change if that vision is going to become reality.

3. Get Confirmation

It's tempting when you have a plan to start implementing it right away. You'll save yourself all kinds of trouble if you'll be patient and avoid that temptation. Share your plans quietly with a few leaders you trust. Get their feedback and make adjustments to your plan.

When you think it's ready, share it with your pastor. You may be the leader of the student ministry, but your pastor is the leader of the church.

Your vision needs to align with your leader's vision. If it doesn't, it's your responsibility to get in alignment, not theirs.

4. Communicate Clearly

Once you have your leader's blessing, it's time to start communicating your vision. Depending on the direction, you may need to give some leaders or students a "heads-up." If the change is significant, you'd be wise to get a handful of influencers on board privately before announcing your plans publicly. Once you've secured the support you need to effectively make the change, begin to communicate the vision down the line, from your leaders to your students.

At this point, I'd like to mention a couple of practical tips. First, your vision should be easy to articulate. If you can't simply and clearly communicate your direction to the group, it's going to be impossible for them to follow it. Get feedback on your presentation from your initial meetings to refine it. Finally, express your vision in positive terms. Admittedly, we often cast vision because things need to change. I'm not saying you should pretend everything is perfect, but as a leader you have to see possibilities where others may not. You should present opportunities where others see only challenge.

With all of these thoughts on vision, you're probably eager to start packing your suitcase. There are a lot of exciting things ahead of you in student ministry, but you'll enjoy the journey a lot more when you tag your luggage. Stand out in a good way, see to it that your character is evident in everything you do, and let your leadership be characterized by a commitment to God's vision.

lightening your load

Don't you hate being the last guy standing after you've boarded the airplane? You know what I'm talking about. Everyone else on the plane is seated, staring forward, as the flight attendant details the safety features of your aircraft. Meanwhile, you're standing in the aisle, engaged in an epic struggle with your carry-on, which refuses to be stowed in the tiny overhead compartment. Beginning to feel self-conscious, you slide the other guy's bag over and throw the paper-thin airline blankets onto your seat to make more room. All the while, you're obstructing others' view of helpful hand motions demonstrating the use of the seatbelt and oxygen mask. You rotate the bag and push harder, giving it everything you've got. The resulting noise competes with the flight attendant, who is now underlining the importance of lighted placards, crewmember instructions, and something about the bathroom smoke detector. By the time the flight attendant finishes her spiel, your bag is stuck, wedged halfway in the compartment. You start to panic as she hangs up the intercom and heads your direction. You know that if you don't get the bag into the bin, she's going to make you check it. And the only things potentially more embarrassing than the little sideshow you've just given to 80 of your newest friends would be: (1) losing the battle after all that effort, or (2) having her effortlessly tap your bag right into the bin, the result of some super-secret stewardess skill.

By some miraculous intervention, you manage to get the bag into the compartment as she walks up to notify you that the "fasten seatbelt" sign is on. Obediently, you sit down, cramming the cheap airline blankets beneath your seat.

As your blood pressure returns to normal, you begin to wonder how in the world you're ever going to get your carry-on back out of the bin. You could wage another public war on your bag or let everyone else deplane before attempting the extraction. It's not that you wanted to break the airline rules by bringing an oversized suitcase on board, but as hard as you tried, you couldn't figure out the mathematical formula the airline provided for determining the appropriate size of your carry-on. What exactly is a linear inch anyway? Most of the time, the real problem isn't linear inches or the size of the overhead compartment (though I've seen bigger glove boxes). Usually, it's a packing problem.

The first thing you need to know about packing is that you can't take everything.

Your suitcase has a finite amount of space and you've got to determine how best to use it. If you're going to have enough room for the items you really need, you're going to have to leave some things behind. That's why the writer to the Hebrews encourages us to "throw off everything that hinders and the sin that so easily entangles," so that we can "run with perseverance the race marked out for us" (12:1). If you're going to carry on in this student ministry journey, you've got to lighten your load so that you can go the distance.

There are two types of things I want to challenge you to leave behind. First are those things that take up too much space. They aren't necessarily bad in and of themselves, but they easily eat up real estate in your carry-on. Second, you should leave behind those things that weigh you down and wear you out.

Super-Sized

One of the things you'll quickly realize in leadership is that you can't be significant everywhere.

Good things become bad things when they keep you from the best things.

Are there good things in your life that are keeping you from greatness in student ministry? What's taking up the most space in your carry-on? Is it media? Do you "unwind" every night in front of the TV, losing hour upon hour, show by show? Is it the Internet? Do you lose track of time on your favorite websites, continually checking that blog or the news? Maybe you're devoting too much suitcase space to sports or recreation. Perhaps it's a hobby that's demanding more and more of your time and money.

There's nothing wrong with any of these things in and of themselves. The issue is how much space you're giving them in your suitcase. The cold, hard fact is that everything you choose to carry takes up space that could be occupied by something else. That doesn't mean you can't watch ESPN or check the news or have a hobby; but you have to understand that when you give your time or energy or money to something, it's no longer available for use in other areas.

This may sound funny, but some youth leaders let time with family or friends take up too much space. Before I elaborate, I want to clarify that I'm talking about a select few youth leaders. Unfortunately, many youth leaders are sacrificing their families on the altar of ministry; I'm not talking about these leaders, who need to take some work out of their carry-on to make room for their family. Some, though have the opposite problem; they have unrealistic expectations about how much time they should be spending with their family or friends.

Your family should be your number one earthly priority; they deserve your attention. Yet, you need to have realistic expectations about what that looks like in practice. Just because you highly value your family doesn't mean that you'll be home every night of the week. I would encourage you to find ways both to involve your family in your ministry and to make quality time for them outside of it. If you're struggling to balance your family and your ministry, let me encourage you to take this chapter to heart on a very practical level. Don't automatically blame the church if your family is getting your leftovers, look in your suitcase. What are you carrying that needs to be left behind?

What I want you to grasp is that the space in your suitcase is valuable, and what you fill it with matters. Be selective. Discern what's best. Leave the good things behind so you have room to pack the best things. You can only read so many books. So which ones will you choose? You can only ingest so much media. What will you watch and what will you listen to? You only have so much time and so much money. How will you spend it? You can only mentor so many students. Which ones will you choose? You can only run so many programs. Which ones deserve your attention?

If you're having a difficult time deciding whether or not to leave something behind, make your decision on the basis of your priorities, not your feelings. You may be very attached to that online Scrabble game or that intramural basketball league or that entire season of your favorite show on DVD. There's a chance you can bring it along, and there's a chance you may have to leave it behind. Before you make your decision, make room for all of your higher priorities. If there's room left over, you may not have to leave it behind. The important thing is that your priorities govern what you pack and what you leave behind.

If you're not sure what your priorities are, start by listing them out. By asking yourself some of the following questions, you'll get a grip on what should get space in your suitcase: What are God's expectations? What are my leader's expectations? What's my God-given vision and mission? What things will need my attention if that vision and mission are to come to pass? What investments of my resources will give me the best return? After you've thought about the answers, I'd encourage you to rank them in order, from most important to least important. Finally, when you've got a list, take some time to decide what you need to do to actually live them out.

My wife, Casey, and I could not be more different when it comes to packing. I would prefer to throw the bare necessities into the smallest possible bag and hit the road. She on the other hand, packs for possibilities. We're only going to be gone for the weekend, but it's possible we could somehow be stranded an extra week, which means we would need to bring more clothing. And if we were there another whole week, we should probably bring some books to read. You never know. And, if we're going to get any reading done, we need to bring more toys to keep the girls entertained. Which reminds me … and before you know it, all we need for our weekend getaway to Branson is a 44-foot U-Haul.

Seriously, the first few times Casey and I traveled together, I wondered if we were ever going to finish packing. It seemed a bit excessive to me. And when we started having kids, the preparation for a trip went to a whole new level. But that's about the time I started appreciating the method behind Casey's madness. On a trip one of the girls gets sick. Not to worry, Casey packed an entire pharmacy! Or one of the girls hasn't stopped crying and fussing for 10 miles. Thankfully, Casey packed just the toy to calm her down. I think I forgot my (you fill in the blank)! Never mind, Casey packed it. It only takes a few incidents like that to give you an appreciation for that kind of preparation.

And yet, there's a balance. After all, you need to be able to get around easily and efficiently. It doesn't do a lot of good to bring something if you can't find it amidst a million other items that you brought along "just in case."

You have to balance portability and performance, and when push comes to shove, you should base your decision on priority.

As you pack for success in student ministry, you have to learn to make the right compromises. Everything can't have your undivided attention. You're going to have to prioritize the packing of some things over others.

Heavy Hitters

Some items should never make the suitcase simply because they will weigh you down and wear you out. My goal isn't to discourage you before you get on the road; I want you to enjoy the journey. If you're lugging any of the following items in your carry-on, it's time to lighten the load.

1. Sin

It's hard to carry on in student ministry when your carry-on is heavy because of sin. There's a reason the writer to the Hebrews encourages us to "throw off everything that hinders and the sin that so easily entangles" (12:1). Sin will keep you from persevering on your journey. If you're trying to carry the weight of some secret sin, you aren't going to make it far. Before long, you'll start making bad decisions, pulling things you really need out of your suitcase to make more room for your quickly growing pet. When your suitcase is full of sin, the first thing that gets thrown by the wayside is your time with God. It's impossible to fit both prayer and continual sin in your carry-on. More times than not, when I talk with a leader who's carrying a suitcase full of compromise, I find that his or her luggage is empty of daily, sincere times with God. When you have a vibrant, ongoing walk with the Lord, you're won't be able to tolerate sin in your suitcase.

As I travel the country and speak, I regularly talk with youth leaders who let some small sin into their suitcase. It wasn't heavy at first. They thought they would be able to manage the load, but before long, they found themselves getting rid of the important things they had packed to make more room for the sin that was now dominating their lives. I can't tell you how many times I've sat across the table from a young man or woman whose life and leadership has been ravaged by the sin in their suitcase. I've looked into the eyes of youth leaders whose families have been ripped apart in the fallout of their moral bankruptcy. They tried to keep sin hidden in their suitcase, but soon it took on a life of its own, and at some point, they lost control. They lost their family. They lost their job. Now, instead of packing for their journey in student ministry, they're packing for a different trip, loading their suitcase with the contents of their office or home.

One reason sin is so lethal is that it "easily entangles." You don't just wake up one day and decide to have an affair with your secretary, it starts with something much more "innocent." Flirting. A phone call after hours. Misusing your expense account wasn't an arbitrary decision to cash in your integrity, it was simply expedience. After all, your family does so much for the church, they must deserve it. It was just one click on the popup, and now you're lugging sexual addiction. It was only a counseling appointment, but you shouldn't have handled it alone; now you're the one with the baggage. You've got to be careful because sin is subtle and progressive. For your own sake, for the sake of your family, for the sake of your ministry, rid your suitcase of any and all sin.

Is there something hidden in some dark pocket or compartment of your carry-on? If you find yourself porting sin around, get rid of it.

Do whatever you need to do to be free.

I would strongly suggest that you go to someone you trust and tell them everything (Proverbs 28:13). Get it all out on the table. No private pleasure could ever compare with the satisfaction of a relationship with Christ unencumbered by sin. Take your sin to Christ, allow Him to lighten your load.

2. Failure

Everyone has experienced failure to one degree or another in their personal lives and in their ministries. If you don't leave yesterday's failures behind, you'll miss out on all that God has for you now and in the future.

I remember making a lot of mistakes as a young leader building a volunteer leadership team. I was zealous about what God was doing in our group and I expected that the volunteers on my team match my passion and commitment. That's all good in theory, but in reality, many of them didn't have the time to devote to the ministry that I had as a part- or full-time employee of the church. I was single at the time, and couldn't figure out why in the world a married father of three working two jobs couldn't give more than 10 hours a week in service to Christ's church? Did he not love God? Did he not care that an entire generation was going to hell in a handbasket?

The last thing I wanted to do was accommodate a bunch of "slackers" who thought they could serve God on their own terms. So, I pretty much asked our volunteers to sign their leadership applications in blood, promising their faithful service for a minimum of 12 months. In addition to the required criminal background check, I also asked them to jump through a few other hoops: giving up their firstborn, for instance. I'm joking, of course. Because of God's grace and the patience of those early volunteers, I'm still friends with many of them today, but I failed on some fronts to lead them effectively.

Today, we have an incredible leadership team of more than 200 committed volunteers. I'm confident that if I wouldn't have left my failures in this area behind, we wouldn't have experienced the growth we have.

You can probably think of an area in your life or leadership where you've failed, or feel like you've failed. Maybe you disappointed a student and they've since given up on God. Perhaps you grew your last youth group from 150 to 15. Your failure doesn't have to be final. What's happened has happened. There's nothing you can do to change it. The important thing is that you grow through it and move beyond it. If you're trying to shoulder the burden of past mistakes, learn from them and then let them go.

3. Comparison

Be careful about comparing yourself to others. God didn't create you or call you to be the leader across town, so don't compare yourself to the leader across town. In the same way, avoid the temptation to compare your ministry to the big youth group across the state or country. What will you gain by sizing yourself up against someone else? In the end, you'll either be discouraged, because you feel like you don't measure up, or you'll be puffed up with pride, because you feel like you're somehow superior.

Comparison is a trap. It will distract you from God's vision by focusing your attention on what's going on around you.

There's nothing wrong with looking around and getting ideas; in fact, we do it at Realife. I love learning from leaders who are doing a great job in student ministry at the local church level. I think of guys like Kevin Moore at Oneighty®, Tom Elmore at L7, or Dan Hunter at Seven Ministries, all of whom have been an encouragement to me in recent months. The important thing is that you don't judge the effectiveness of your ministry by comparing your results to someone else's. There are all kinds of factors involved that you're probably not taking into account, not the least of which is the fact that you're not called to be the same. Chances are, if you're always busying yourself looking to this leader or that model, you're neglecting areas that actually do need your attention. Your journey is your own. Be who God is calling you to be and leave comparison behind.

4. Perfectionism

Some leaders will have to leave perfectionism behind. There's nothing wrong with excellence or high standards. In fact, we could use a lot more excellence in student ministry, so if you happen to be a sloppy leader, this thought is not an excuse for your mediocrity. If you're a perfectionist, on the other hand, I want to encourage you not to make excuses either. You may be inclined to perfectionism, either by your personality or your experiences. I'm not suggesting you change your personality; I'm encouraging you to not let it limit you.

This leadership journey is often fast and furious. Perfectionists often end up devoting way too much energy to things that, in the end, aren't all that important, while the things that are truly important slip right through their fingers. Perfectionism isn't all bad; it can be used to your advantage. The issue is knowing which things are worth your critical eye or attention to detail and which things aren't. Don't major in the minors; leave perfectionism behind or it will weigh you down.

5. Selfish Ambition

There's never room for selfish ambition in your suitcase. Impure motives are heavy (and they've been known to set off the metal detector). If you're using student ministry as a stepping stone or a platform for personal attention or advancement, you're not going to take the group anywhere. You may feel better about yourself or advance your career in the process, but at some point you won't be able to bear the weight of the selfish ambition you're dragging behind you.

Impure motives flesh themselves out in a number of ways in student ministry. Often, a temptation for youth pastors is to leave their group when the grass seems greener on the other side. It's not that you have to be a youth pastor for your entire life, but few youth leaders are erring on that side of the issue. Most leave student ministry too soon.

Like the power of compound interest, your influence multiplies the longer you stay in one place.

Don't leave because it's easier than staying or because something "better" comes your way. Longevity is best for you and your students.

One of the things I appreciate about Eric Porter, Realife's junior high director, is his longevity. Eric has been with us for 6 years now, which is incredible in student ministry. As a leader, I can't begin to tell you how much it means to have someone I can count on overseeing such an important aspect of our ministry. What's really fun to watch is how Eric's faithfulness has impacted the rest of the group. Not only is our junior high ministry effective, our high school ministry is healthier today because of the consistent example and leadership Eric gave those students in their critical junior high years.

6. Personal Preference

A lot of leaders get bogged down by personal preference. Be careful about making leadership decisions on the basis of what you're comfortable with or what you would prefer, rather than on what's biblical or best for your group. Hopefully, you're a leader in student ministry because you want to take kids on a journey with Christ, not because you want to build a program that appeals to your sensibilities.

I've been really impressed to watch John Lindell lead change over the years without regard for personal preference. Time after time, I've watched him make decisions based on what's right for the church, even when it meant moving out of his comfort zone personally. God has used his selfless, courageous leadership to make an incredible impact on our congregation and community.

This issue is really practical. Pay attention to what other people think. Don't rush to make decisions because you want to make a change. Don't fail to make decisions because you are more comfortable with the status quo. From time to time, get a focus group together. Have some of your students or leaders tell you what they really think about this or that. I'm not advocating leadership by consensus. Don't take a vote over every leadership decision, or decide what to do or not to do on the basis of majority rule. The important thing is keeping your finger on the pulse of your ministry, making decisions on the basis of what's best for all involved, rather than on what you'd prefer to do.

This list isn't exhaustive. There may be other things unique to your personality or experience that you need to let go of. For example, I remember when I realized that I had to leave sarcasm behind because it was putting a lid on my effectiveness as a leader. As a relatively new youth pastor, I would use humor to build relationships with students. I would joke with a student about something and they might make a sarcastic comment back. Not one to be one-upped, I'd respond by making an even more sarcastic comment. We'd banter back and forth until one of us would finally give up. To this day, I remember the time I crushed a student with my sarcasm. I could see it in his face and it forever changed the dynamic of our relationship. I realized that I wasn't winning in student ministry by "winning" a sarcastic exchange with a student. Today, I use humor to relate to students, but I'm not sarcastic. I took sarcasm out of my suitcase a long time ago.

Lighten the Load

Allow the Lord to show you what things He wants you to leave behind to make room for the things you really need. Lighten your load; you'll be glad you did.

In the next chapter, we're going to be looking at some of the things you need to pack for success in student ministry. Before you move on, take an inventory of your carry-on. Are you being weighed down by things you were never meant to carry? Are there items that are keeping you from being effective by crowding out the things you need? There's only so much you can carry, so leave the junk behind.

packing your bag

A few years ago, I went on a ministry trip to Kansas City, where I was preaching at a youth leaders' conference hosted by my good friend Bill Kirkpatrick. Two of my interns at the time, Scott and Ryan (nicknames Wisk and Wake, respectively), were along for the ride. Wisk has a fairly decent track record at home, but let's just say he tends to forget things when he's out of his element. In fact, we've traveled together a number of times and I honestly don't remember a single trip where he managed to get everything he needed into his suitcase.

At any rate, the details of what I'm about to share are a little sketchy—not because they are untrue, but because there's no way I could possibly remember everything Wisk forgot that weekend.

It all started in the Braum's drive-thru. We hadn't even left town, when he yells from the backseat.

"Can you make that shake a malt?"

I quickly corrected the order: "Actually, can you make the sha–"

"Shoot!" Wisk interjected.

"Hold on a minute ..." Confused, I turned around, "So do you want a shake or a malt?"

"A malt. It's just ... I think I left my bag in my car back at the church," he said, frantically flipping through our belongings in hope of a miracle.

"Wisk! You're joking, right? We're already going to be late! There's no way we can drive 30 minutes back to the church to get your stuff," I explained.

"I'll be good," Wisk surrendered to reality, accustomed to making do without.

Wisk had forgotten things before, but never his entire bag. I could tell we were in for a memorable trip. And I was right. After the service that night, the three of us were talking in my hotel room, which happened to be on the 14th floor. Wisk was supposed to have brought my back medication up from the car along with a handful of other items.

"Wisk, where'd you put my medicine?" I asked.

He hesitated. Laughing, I started joking, "You left it in the car, didn't you? First your clothes, now my medicine!"

Here's where it gets good. Wisk managed to get all the way down to the first floor before realizing he forgot the car keys in his room. So he came all the way back up to the 14th floor, picked up the keys and went all the way back down to the first floor, where he had to switch elevators to get access to the parking lot. Ten minutes passed and then my phone rang.

"Hello?" I laughed, noticing Wisk's name on the caller ID.

"Hey man, I've got your medicine, but I forgot my hotel key in your room and now I can't get back into the hotel!"

And so ended day one of our three-day extravaganza.

When you're traveling, few things are as frustrating as arriving at your destination only to realize that you forgot something really important.

The journey in student ministry is a lot of fun, but it's also demanding, and that's why it's important that you're prepared for the trip. You've tagged your luggage and lightened your load; it's time to start packing.

The Essentials

Regardless of your destination, there are some things you should always pack. It doesn't matter if you're going overseas for six months or if you're going across the state for six days, you've got to have "the essentials." I suppose it's possible to survive without clothing, deodorant, a toothbrush and toothpaste, but doing so is not exactly a formula for success.

We're all different and the definition of "essential" seems to vary from person to person. Some people can get by with little more than a toothbrush and a change of underwear. Others, though, wouldn't dare travel without a very specific list of must-haves— their iPod, or a handful of magazines, or a hair dryer in case the one stuck to the wall at the hotel doesn't work. Most people pack their essentials in their carry-on, so that they're prepared in the increasingly likely event that their luggage is lost in transit.

Whatever your style, there are some things you should never be without on this journey in student ministry, regardless of where the road takes you. Pack the following items first. They are non-negotiable—essentials for success in student ministry.

1. Spiritual Character

First and foremost, you've got to pack authentic spirituality. As a youth pastor, you're not just any leader; you're a spiritual leader. Remember, you reproduce what you are. If you expect students to walk with God, you have to walk with Him. Don't just point the

way; bring them along on the journey, leading by example.
It's unfortunate, but far too many youth leaders get their suitcases
stuffed with every imaginable resource.

When the bag starts to get too heavy or they get too busy, the first thing they pull out to lighten the load is their walk with God.

Does that make any sense whatsoever? Of course it doesn't; it's
completely irrational. But youth leaders across the country do it
every day. Content to operate on the fumes of some past experience
with God, they rely on their own resources rather than receiving
God's. Be careful not to run on "empty" spiritually; it's one of the
surest ways to burn out or fall into compromise.

The work we're called to do as youth leaders is beyond our natural
abilities. I don't care how cool you are or where you went to school
or what experiences you've had. All of those things combined and
multiplied by a million won't begin to scratch the surface in student
ministry. Sure, your group may grow numerically, or you may have
a great event here or there, but remember, those are just stops
on your journey. You're after something more; you want to see
students experience the abundant life of Christ. I love what author
George MacDonald said: "In everything we do without God, we
must fail miserably, or succeed more miserably." You can exert more
and more effort in the flesh, but you'll end up exhausted and dried
up. Spirit produces spirit and flesh produces flesh.

Your ministry should simply be an overflow of your relationship with God.

That's why I always tell our volunteers that who you are is more important than what you do. Who you are on the inside directly affects every aspect of your life and leadership on the outside. Are you operating out of the abundance of your walk with Christ, or are you spiritually scraping by, hoping your students do what you say and not what you do?

Two obvious, but important ways you can develop spiritual character as a leader are through prayer and the study of God's Word. First, pack your prayer list and spend time daily seeking God. Whatever you're facing, the battle is won in prayer. Pray for God to lead you. Pray for your events. Second, pack your Bible, read it daily (and not just to get some sermon out of it), and memorize it. Remember that God's Word is what changes lives.

One of the traps youth leaders can fall into is replacing their personal time with God with sermon prep time. The old two-in-one trick. Every time you go and study the Bible, you're looking for sermons rather than listening to God. One discipline I've put in place really helps me keep my priorities straight spiritually in ministry. I refuse to work on any message or teaching unless I've spent personal time in prayer and the Word. When I'm tempted to begin working on a sermon before spending that time, I'm reminded that I need my own heart to be full, that my ministry is an overflow of my relationship with Christ. The cool thing

I've found is that when you prioritize that time with Jesus, your effectiveness as a minister of the gospel is significantly heightened. If you want to be effective, you can't afford not to be in God's presence daily.

Whatever your daily routine looks like, don't get stuck in a rut. Keep it fresh. That might mean that one day you spend more time journaling, but the next, you devote more attention to worship. From time to time, you might take a walk in the park and reflect on God's attributes. At other times, you'll find yourself spending more time meditating on the Scriptures. Experiment with the variety of spiritual disciplines that will help you cultivate an intimate walk with Christ.

In Ecclesiastes, Solomon wisely observes that when your axe is dull, you have to work harder (10:10).

The cool thing about incorporating the spiritual disciplines into your life is that, by doing so, you sharpen your spiritual axe. The result is effective ministry. You don't have to make things happen in the flesh, because you're operating in the power of the Spirit, walking in God's wisdom and power.

2. Teachable Spirit

One of the most important qualities of any leader is a teachable spirit. You don't have to know everything, but if you pack a teachable spirit, there's no end to what God will do through you.

I'm talking about a posture of the heart where you're open and receptive to all of the things you might learn from God, life and the people around you.

When you act like you have it all figured out, you place a limit on your leadership potential. I have the opportunity to travel and speak to youth leaders across the country fairly regularly. After I speak, I try to interact with as many youth leaders as possible on an individual basis. One of the first things I notice very quickly in a conversation is whether or not the person I'm speaking with has a teachable spirit. Some leaders are obviously hungry to learn and ask insightful questions and listen intently (not that my thoughts are all that, I'm talking about the spirit of the person). On the other hand, some barely say hello before they start delineating their accomplishments and the top 10 reasons they're going to be the next rock star youth pastor.

It doesn't matter how big your group is, or how popular it is, or how multi-talented you are, there's always more you can learn. Since you know you don't have all the answers, maintain a disposition that reflects an understanding that God may want to teach you something at any moment, in any conversation. Don't be the one whose mouth is always open, sharing your latest revelations from on high. One of the things I respect about my friend Andy Braner is that, even though he's busy writing books and running camps for thousands of students, he never stops learning. Whenever we interact, I'm impressed by all of the life lessons he picks up in his everyday experiences. Be like Andy. Take time to listen to the people God has placed around you and you'll be more effective as a result.

Another thing to keep in mind as it relates to a teachable spirit is that you reap what you sow. One of the cool things about having a teachable spirit is that it rubs off on those around you, so when you have to teach a principle or correct someone, you're likely to get a favorable response because that's the kind of spirit you've modeled.

3. Loyal Heart

A loyal heart is another essential for student ministry. As a leader on an occasionally difficult journey, it is refreshing to be surrounded by a loyal support system.

If you've got a loyal team behind you, big challenges seem small.

But even little incidents are a big deal when you have the added stress of your own team working against you.

In the same way, you can refresh your pastor or leader by being faithful and loyal. The church as a whole is a lot more complicated than just your one department, and your pastor needs (and deserves) to know that he can count on you representing him well at all times. I'm blessed to have an incredible leader in John Lindell, Lead Pastor at James River Assembly. When you have as much love and respect for your leader as I do for my pastor, it's easy to be loyal. And yet, I recognize that not every pastor is a John Lindell. Regardless, the principle remains the same, whether or not it's easy for you as a leader.

Loyalty means that you support your leader not just in their presence, but especially in their absence. Look for opportunities to publicly align yourself with your leader and their vision. When it becomes necessary, defend your leader. If someone comes up to you and wants to gripe about your leader and you're unfamiliar with the situation, take the opportunity to teach that person about the importance of unity within the body of Christ. When you have opportunity later, inform your leader about what happened, how you addressed it, and what, if anything, they'd like you to do to follow up.

Loyalty doesn't mean that you will agree with your leader 100% of the time. You may find yourself in a situation where you would be happy if you agreed with your pastor even 50% of the time. Loyalty means that when you do occasionally disagree, you're willing to move past your personal preference out of respect for your leader and his authority. Maybe it's difficult for you to be loyal to your leader, because you feel like you don't even know him. He's not a mentor to you. You've never even been invited to his home to share a meal. As difficult and real as these challenges are for some leaders, they shouldn't affect your loyalty.

If God has called you to a church, He's called you to serve its leader.

If you can't manage to find alignment with your leader or if you are in disagreement about something that you feel is a deal-breaker, you need to move on. If you do choose to leave, do so gracefully and with integrity. Otherwise, as a member of his team, you need to get in line with his heart and vision. Your leader deserves the full support of his team.

4. Responsible Approach

Another must-pack essential for student ministry is responsibility, which makes me think back to one of our spring retreats. At the time, we had about 500 students in the group. One of our volunteers was in charge of "the jelly relay." All of our students were lined up in teams of 20 and each team had a kiddy pool filled with jelly. One at a time, as fast as they could, the students had to plunge their heads into the grape jelly cesspool, inhaling as much of it into their mouths as possible before running down the field and spitting it into their team's jar. The first team to fill up their jar won 10,000 points. At the time, we also allowed certain leaders to give students points at their discretion. We later abandoned that policy, for reasons you're about to see (and because some leaders would offer students points to be their indentured servants all weekend, but that's another story for another book).

So the students are dunking, running, spitting; dunking, running, spitting. Finally, one of the teams manages to fill their jar and is declared the victor. As they're awarded their 10,000 points, the volunteer leader over the game rotation has an epiphany. Before all of the cheering dies down, his bullhorn roars:

"Alright, listen up! I'll give 5,000 bonus points to the team of the first person to drink their entire jar of jelly!"

The kids scream enthusiastically. Almost in slow motion, the bravest students jog to the jars, their flags waving and teammates cheering in the background. Pause. Now, in the moment, this leader is thinking, "This is the best idea. The kids love this!" In fact, this leader wasn't thinking responsibly. Fast-forward and play.

The kids run in the heat to their next scheduled game on the rotation, which happens to be poolside. All is well—except for the handful of students vomiting grape jelly into the swimming pool—which, for the record, puts a bit of a damper on the pool games.

I've met youth leaders before who eat this kind of stuff up (sorry for the disturbing mental picture). In fact, they almost view an event as a failure unless a student throws up: "You had nine kids puking!? Dude, that's incredible! Teenagers love this stuff!"

Now, I can attest to the fact that the brains of teenagers have not fully developed, but I don't know many teenagers whose idea of a good time is throwing up large volumes of grape jelly ... in the swimming pool ... in front of their friends ... each of whom had a part in liquefying said jelly before orally transporting it to the jar from which it was drunk. Granted, there may be one sick puppy here or there (every group has at least one of these kids), who actually *would* want to hurl grape jelly into a swimming pool repeatedly, just for the fun of it. But that's all the more reason why you, as the leader, have to be responsible to draw the line for your students.

Even if you think watching nine kids puke grape jelly into the swimming pool is funny, just wait until you get a phone call from the guy who cleans the pool.

Or from nine angry parents, one of whom is a powerful attorney and whose daughter happens to be seriously allergic to high fructose corn syrup. All of a sudden, responsibility looks pretty attractive, even if it means having to make a decision that isn't popular in the excitement of the moment.

Being responsible means thinking things through. Is this best for the students? Is this best for the church? Will this cultivate my credibility with parents? Will it build trust with my leader? Anyone can have fun, but as the leader, you have to be responsible.

As the leader, you are responsible for all of the activities associated with the student ministry. That doesn't mean you have to do everything personally. It means that the buck stops with you. You're responsible to God and to your leader for your job description, whatever it looks like and however often it changes. You're responsible for the spiritual atmosphere of your worship service, for preparing a message that's grounded in God's Word, for making sure the building is clean after that big event, for bringing all of the students back from the retreat in one piece. You often get the credit when things go well (even if you're not directly responsible), and you take the heat when things go south (even if it's not your fault).

In student ministry, it's easy to get caught up in the excitement of the moment, but as the leader, you have to remember to keep a level head at all times. I hope as a youth leader you have plenty of fun in student ministry, but I can tell you from experience that it's a lot easier to have fun when you've been responsible—when you've done your homework and things are running smoothly.

Everything Else

Once you've got the essentials in the suitcase, everything else you pack depends on where you're going and what you're doing when you get there. What's the climate like at the church where you work or volunteer? Is it a church plant reaching young professionals or a 100-year-old congregation with mostly 100-year-old congregants? Is the ethnic makeup of your church diverse or homogeneous? What is your congregation's history? What about the student ministry's?

You've got to ask yourself what your leader's expectations are. What is his personality like? What is his vision for the church? What are his goals? What kind of culture is he trying to create and how does he plan on doing so? Is his approach event-driven or more organic? What does he highly value?

What are the students in your ministry like? Do you have a diverse group or do you have 90% homeschool students? Are your students geographically concentrated around the church, or are they spread out in rural areas? Have your students been raised in church or are they first-generation Christians? What is the level of their spiritual maturity? Do they have Internet access at home? What do they like to do for fun?

The demographics of your community are also important to know as you pack your bags. Your approach in a blue-collar community in an area that's economically depressed is going to be radically different from one in an affluent community characterized by corporate careers. Is your congregation in the heart of the heartland or is it right on the coast?

What you pack doesn't just depend on where you're going, but also on what you're doing when you get there. Are you a full-time youth pastor with a salary and benefits and a $50,000 annual youth budget? Or are you holding down three part-time jobs and volunteering with the youth group on the side? If you are on staff, what's your job description? Do you have the luxury of focusing all your efforts on the student ministry or are you also overseeing children or music?

I often talk to youth leaders who know it's important to pack for the journey, but they do so haphazardly.

They're in such a hurry to get to the gate that they quickly grab some things they think they'll need, throw them in the bag, and hit the road. And that's really unfortunate, because it's backwards. As part of the preparation for Realife's first missions trip, I took a pre-trip to our destination, which happened to be Jamaica (sounds rough, I know). It was pretty rough, actually, because I failed to think about the fact that I was going to a tropical climate when I packed for the trip. I stepped off the plane into sweltering 90 degree heat wearing a sweater and carrying a bag full of clothing well-suited to Springfield winters. Always start your journey with the end in mind.

Rethinking Relevance

You could really sum up this idea of packing appropriately for your destination in one word—relevance. Unfortunately, "relevance" has become an overused buzzword in student ministry. If you don't think of the magazine, you probably think of cutting-edge ministry—a smoke-filled stage, a drama set to secular music, a youth pastor "relating to the kids" through the underestimated medium of profanity. Those ideas reflect an unfortunate, if inaccurate, understanding of relevance.

As youth leaders, we often think of relevance on a surface level only. We'll invest all of our time and money in making something look good or packaging it in just the right way. Take an outreach event as an example. You design sharp tickets and flyers promoting that you're going to be giving away the latest game system or Apple product. The kids show up and everything looks cool. And that's the extent of your thinking on "relevance." That's all well and good, but what really needs to be thought through are the deliverables of the event. Are they relevant to a student and to your goal? Relevance is more about substance than it is about style.

Let me mention a few things that are really relevant. One would be

God. Don't water down the faith you represent in order
to "connect."

What could be more relevant to lost humanity than the fact that God wants a relationship with us and He's gone to incredible lengths to make that possible?

We're talking about kids who come from broken families. The idea
of being adopted into God's family is incredibly relevant. Don't you
think God's power to free someone from an addiction is well-suited
to the student who finds himself addicted to meth? Your choice of
a secular music clip at the beginning of your message doesn't come
close to the relevance of that reality.

Several years ago, one of my associates was using a clip from the
movie *E.T.* as an opening illustration for his Sunday School lesson.
The guy in the AV booth hit play right on cue, but was delayed
several seconds pressing stop. The video played well into the next
scene, stopping right after the scene's profanity-laced climax.
Imagine Mom and Dad's surprise when they asked their 6th grader
what they learned in class and the response was an expletive.

What about simplicity? When a student is lured to your youth
group by that fancy ticket, do you have people at the doors to
welcome them and point them in the right direction? You have
them fill out an information card so you can follow up. Have you

thought through how to make that process as simple and user-friendly as possible? Is it easy for students to get to your retreat or plugged into your small group program?

How about love? Every single week I have interaction with students who are starved for love. Jesus said that people will know we're Christians by our love (John 13:35). Essentially, he's saying that love is incredibly relevant. Is the love of Christ one of your ministry's hallmarks? When visitors show up at your doorstep, do they sense the love of God through their interaction with the students and leaders in your group?

I've just mentioned a few suggestions here and you can probably think of several more. As you do identify ways you can truly connect with a teenager, I would encourage you to think practically. There isn't a one-size-fits-all approach to relevance, as if the banners in your youth room make you relevant. Great if your room is appealing; it should be, but if everything it represents doesn't work to reach a student, you're missing it. The reason I mentioned all of the questions above was to help you think very specifically about your student ministry. The way you show love in the inner city may look a little different from the approach the other guy is taking in the suburbs.

You may have everything looking great on paper, but if it doesn't work within the context of your congregation or community, it won't work.

So what should you pack specifically? I would encourage you
to pack the skills and resources you need to be relevant to your
church, to your leader, to your students and to their parents. If
your church places a lot of emphasis on the youth service, you
are going to want to prioritize your growth as a communicator. If
your church's approach is more organic, you'll want to pack good
interpersonal skills that will help you effectively lead individuals
and smaller groups. If your church highly values excellence in your
communication materials, you'd better pack some proofreading
skills. If your entire student ministry is into video games, bust out
the Xbox. If the last youth pastor didn't pay attention to details
and rubbed a lot of parents the wrong way, pack the attention
to detail and communication skills you'll need to overcome that
challenge.

Be relevant. Don't feel pressured to pack like the youth pastor with
the big national ministry. His suitcase won't work where you're
going. Whatever you pack, make sure it's appropriate for
your destination.

following the rules

As a student, Tony had a lot of influence, and was using it to cause trouble in the group. It seems like we had a standing weekly appointment; I would confront his behavior, he would blow me off, and nothing would change. With a youth retreat right around the corner, I had been praying that Tony would go and get things right with God. When I found out he signed up, I was thrilled. Well, kind of. I was glad he was going, but wasn't looking forward to inevitable daily confrontations.

I was so excited when Tony responded to a salvation invitation, giving his heart to Christ at the end of one of the retreat services.

It was a picture-perfect conversion, complete with tears, snot, and hugs that left tears and snot on your shirt.

Determined to establish a fresh start, I wanted to challenge Tony in his new relationship with God, so I pulled him aside after he had finished praying.

"I'm so proud of you for making that decision to follow Jesus!"

"Thanks, Pastor Scotty."

"Listen man, I know I've had to come down on you quite a bit lately. I've been confronting you because I care about you and want what's best for you."

"I know, Pastor Scotty. I appreciate it."

"Good. Listen man, you just made a decision for God. Did you mean that?"

"Definitely," he replied with confidence.

"That's so cool! I want to encourage you to start living out your faith. You know that means you're going to have to start acting differently, right?"

"Yes sir," he responded, smiling.

"Good." I smiled back. "I don't want to have to keep knocking you over the head, but I'm going to hold you accountable to this decision."

"Sounds good," he said, giving me a big hug before going back to the altar to pray with some of his friends.

Those are the moments you live for in student ministry. I was really encouraged by the change I saw in Tony. The next day we loaded all of the kids on the bus and prepared to leave. Before we left, I checked with the volunteer overseeing the head count.

"Are we ready to roll out of here?" I asked.

"Yeah, we've got all 76 kids. But there is one problem …"

"What's that?" I asked.

"Well, it's Tony. I moved him to the front of the bus because he was trying to get fresh with Amanda during the head count. I told him there was no PDA, but he wouldn't listen and …" I walked away mid-conversation and made a beeline for the bus.

"Come here, Tony!" I said with a disgusted look on my face as I boarded the bus.

"Wha–" he began to ask.

"You know what! I said, 'come here'!"

Tony stepped off the bus and I proceeded to let him have it.

"Did last night mean anything to you at all? You were crying at the altar. You told me you wanted to change. And now 12 hours later, you're trying to put the moves on Amanda and disrespecting one of my leaders. You know there's no PDA at retreat and I thought you were done with the rebellious attitude!"

Sheepishly, Tony tried to calm me down, "Pastor Scotty ..."

"Save it, Tony. Don't 'Pastor Scotty' me! Do you think you can play games with God? When you play games with God, you lose. Don't be a loser! Now get back on the bus, we'll talk when we get back to the church." I started to walk away, my verbal tirade complete.

"But, Pastor Scotty ..."

"Get back on the bus, Tony!" I raised my voice without turning around. About that time, the volunteer who informed me of the whole situation ran up to me, clipboard in hand and a distressed look on her face.

"I hate to tell you this, Pastor Scotty ..."

"What now?" I asked.

"It was the other Tony."

As the buses began leaving for the church, I wanted to throw myself beneath one of them. The good news is that Tony forgave me. After retreat, I held him accountable for walking with Christ and he held me accountable for not being a knucklehead.

Close Call

When you travel, your bag isn't just your business. If you're going to make it very far on this journey in student ministry, you're going to have to allow others to inspect your luggage from time to time.

No one likes going through security at the airport. It's inconvenient to say the least. All of your personal effects are sprawled out in Tupperware bins. You have to remove your laptop from your bag, take off your shoes and your belt. You place your keys and cell phone in the little bowl, hoping and praying that you don't trip the metal detector because you know it's a one-way ticket to additional-screening-ville. And that invariably involves the wand treatment and the pat-down.

In that moment, when you are randomly selected for additional screening and the lady is wiping your laptop down with a little gauze pad on the end of a stick that subtly resembles Bob Barker's microphone on *The Price Is Right*, you have to remember that the rules are there to protect you. The reality is that there are real threats to your safety. There are people who are fanatically dedicated to the planning and carrying out of attacks on American citizens. When you actually stop and think about what happened on 9/11—and I'm not talking about the 9/11 that's been reduced to a slogan on a bumper sticker or a talking point on conservative radio, I'm talking about planes loaded with American citizens slamming into people's workplaces, resulting in the death of thousands, and forever changing the way we look at the world— when you think about that, it gives you a perspective and an appreciation for security. It may not be convenient, but it's there for your benefit and for the benefit of those around you.

As a leader, you have an enemy who would like nothing more than to destroy you and your ministry. He wants to slip something into your bag when you're not looking. You may not even notice it at first, but in the end, it could do untold damage to you and everyone around you. That's why accountability is so important; you need someone you trust to look through your luggage and hold you accountable for its contents.

My parents had my youngest brother, William, later in life. With 16 years between us, I've had the unique privilege of being his older brother and his youth pastor. Recently, the two of us were flying together; when we arrived at the security checkpoint at the airport, William put his carry-on on the conveyor belt and began to take off his shoes.

In my head, everything that follows in this story is set to suspenseful music, like the soundtrack from William Shatner's *Rescue 911*.

As William walked through the metal detector, several TSA agents gathered around his bag. Before long, they were joined by airport police and unidentified officers dressed completely in black. My first thought was that the whole thing was some kind of joke, but as I watched the authorities systematically unpack my brother's bag, I realized it was the real deal. My second thought was about where I could have gone wrong. As William's older brother and youth pastor, we'd talked about all kinds of things over the years, but never terrorism. How could I have missed the warning signs?

It turns out William had a bullet in his shaving kit. He didn't remember putting it there, but it was left over from a hunting trip he'd taken a few months prior. Fortunately, the situation was diffused when one of the officers recognized me and convinced his colleagues to call off the hounds, insisting we were neither terrorists nor crazed gunmen. To my brother's credit, he handled the situation very well even though it was a major inconvenience. He recognized the officers were simply doing their jobs; they wanted to keep everyone safe.

The Power of the Red Sweater

Packing according to the rules starts with a healthy respect for authority. Whether or not you like it, the man with the magnetic wand is an authority in your life. It doesn't matter if you like him or her, or if you think you could do their job better; the security screener's maroon TSA sweater indicates their position of authority over you. That authority gives them the right to hold you accountable for how you pack. You can reject the TSA's authority, but you should be prepared to accept the consequences if you do.

Similarly, your pastor or leader is an authority whom God has placed in your life. There is an umbrella of protection on your life when you submit yourself to that authority. Submitting isn't always convenient or expedient, but in the end you'll always be blessed for doing so.

As a youth leader, you should have a grasp on this issue because you're an authority to the students and volunteer leaders in your ministry.

If you want them to line up behind your leadership, model a respect for authority in your service to your leader. After all, you reap what you sow.

Better Safe Than Sorry

Accountability naturally flows from authority. It is the screener's authority that gives them the right to inspect your bags. When you have respect for that authority and the resulting accountability, it changes the way you pack.

As a leader, you need to give a friend that you trust authority in your life to hold you to a high standard of accountability. God didn't intend for us to be self-sufficient. The student ministry journey is a lot more enjoyable when you've got someone to share it with. And the cool thing about accountability is that you don't just share the joy of the good times, you share the load in the hard times.

Be careful not to approach accountability like it's some intrusive obligation. Give your accountability partner complete and open access to your heart and life. Invite them in, don't make them pry for information. You probably know someone who didn't give anyone access to their luggage, who tried to get around security. It was more convenient in the moment, but was incredibly inconvenient in the end. Often, the people who skip security aren't the ones who get hurt the most; it's all of the innocent people around them.

I have such an appreciation for my friend Darin Poe—not only is he my district youth director, but he's also my accountability partner. Whether Darin and I are sitting down over coffee or talking on the phone, I can count on him asking me how I'm doing with God. He cares enough to ask me about my family life. He listens when I talk about Realife. Through thick and thin, I know I can count on Darin to be there with an encouraging word, a listening ear, or a challenging thought. I'm privileged to do the same for him. We're both better leaders because we've safeguarded our lives with accountability.

Some may think that I go overboard, but I take accountability seriously; some might call it "hardcore." While Darin is my primary accountability partner, I've got other layers of accountability in my life. When it comes to accountability, I'm of the opinion that you can't get too much. From my lead pastor to my staff, my friends to my family, I count on the people God has placed in my life to sharpen and challenge me. As an example, I regularly tell my staff that I want to hear from them if they see anything in my life that concerns them, whether it's a bad attitude, a questionable conversation, or a poor decision.

I love the security and support I get having accountability above, beside, and beneath me. Surround yourself with accountability.

There are different kinds of accountability, and I would recommend two in particular. First, you need personal accountability. Find someone who's committed to regularly looking in your luggage. It should be someone you trust and someone who isn't afraid to tell you the truth. They can help you see when the things you've packed are in a state of disarray, when you're not prioritizing your walk with God or when you're struggling in an area. And as an objective outside voice, they can help you see what you need to do to get things back on track.

You also need professional accountability, someone who will push you to hit the mark in ministry. As a leader, you should have someone holding you responsible for ministry outcomes or results. Most likely, your pastor has expectations for your performance as a leader, and hopefully you have goals of your own. It would be wise of you to share those expectations and goals with someone who will challenge you to achieve them, someone you can bounce ideas off of and who will encourage you when things aren't going so well.

I've found that a healthy accountability relationship has four key ingredients:

1. Trust

If your accountability relationship is going to do you any good, you have to trust your accountability partner. You're never going to open up to someone if you are worried that they're going to be airing your dirty laundry in the church parking lot as soon as you're done meeting or as soon as they decide they don't like you anymore. It's important that you trust your friend's ability to keep a confidence.

It's also important that you trust your accountability partner's spiritual character. Don't choose someone who is going to cause you to lower your standards. There was a time when I met with a guy who didn't challenge me. If I was struggling with something, his response would be something like, "It's OK, Scotty. We all struggle and God is gracious." I didn't need someone to tell me that humanity is depraved or that God is good; I knew that. I needed someone who would challenge me to pursue God passionately. That's why we don't meet anymore. Be careful about being accountable to someone who will cause you to rationalize mediocrity; it will only give you a false sense of security.

2. Honesty

For this kind of relationship to work, you both have to be committed to honesty. In fact, that's kind of the point. If you're not being completely honest with your accountability partner, you're doing little more than fulfilling some empty religious duty.

Effective accountability confronts who you really are, not who you'd like to be, so be open and transparent.

3. Consistency

In an airport, you have little choice but to go through security, but in life, it's easy to get sloppy with accountability. Work to establish a pattern. How often will you meet? When and where? What are your goals for the relationship? Are you holding one another accountable generally or are you focusing on a specific issue or struggle? What approach will you take? What questions will you ask one another? Will you read a book together and discuss it? Once you set a meeting time, guard it. When things are going well, don't bail on your accountability partner, thinking you don't need the meeting. Meet anyway. Your friend may need your perspective or help. You'll stay on the offensive and reinforce an important habit for success in student ministry.

4. Responsibility

In and of itself, an accountability meeting is a time-out to pull aside and talk about life. It's only talk, though, unless you take personal responsibility for your actions outside of the meeting. One of the things I've found to be helpful is establishing consequences in the event that you violate your commitment. For instance, I've told Darin that if I'm struggling with something and don't address it appropriately, he needs to contact my pastor to get him involved.

Your actions have consequences and your accountability should reflect that reality. It would be much better to establish self-imposed consequences than to come to a place where you experienced consequences that are beyond your control. As much as I would prefer that my pastor not have to get involved in a situation where I was struggling, that would be far better than the alternative. Don't be content to go through some routine; be proactive in your pursuit of personal growth day in and day out.

Safety First

Everyone goes through security. There aren't exceptions. If you're unwilling to let an authority look through your luggage, it means one of three things: you have a problem with authority, you're not willing to be held accountable for your actions, or you have something to hide. In any of those cases, you're limiting how far you'll go on your student ministry journey.

As a leader, you will win when you pack according to the rules. Embrace authority and accountability; they'll keep you on the right path.

flying frequently

Traveling is one of those things that loses its novelty when you do it regularly. Don't get me wrong. I love visiting different places and seeing different people. It's the actual process of getting from one place to the next that tends to get old after a while. When you first start traveling, even the process is fun. Maybe you remember your first flight on an airplane or the first time you traveled to another country. You listened intently to the flight attendant's discourse on safety, reviewing the safety features of your aircraft on the little card in the seatback in front of you. You looked forward to the layover because it gave you the opportunity to explore a strange airport. You thought it was so cool to get a bag of pretzels and half a can of Coke halfway through the flight. At first, traveling is an exciting adventure, but after a few trips it seems more like a means to an end.

It won't take long for the novelty to wear off of your student ministry journey. At some point, the honeymoon will end and the reality of what it is you're called to do will set in. Unfortunately, this is the point where a lot of leaders get discouraged and give up. Youth group isn't all the fun and games they thought it would be. There are times in student ministry when you're going to be tired, when there's more to do than you feel like you could handle in a million lifetimes. You're going to encounter people you'd rather not encounter. There will be situations you'd rather not face. When you come to that point, you have a decision to make. Will I be a frequent flyer? Will I be a road warrior? Or will I give up?

Remember, you have an ultimate destination, and it will be well worth whatever difficulty you encounter along the way.

There are going to be incredible milestones on your journey toward that ultimate destination. Those things are all exciting, but there's also going to be a lot of traveling involved in going from milestone to milestone, ultimately reaching your destination. There are times when the last thing I want to do is spend half of my day in airplanes and airports, but then I get to my destination and I forget about the relatively minor difficulties or inconveniences I encountered to get there. Traveling isn't an end in and of itself. It's a means to other ends. And yet, that doesn't mean traveling isn't important.

There have been times when I've sat through a really long flight and wished I was as prepared for the trip as the guy next to me, the frequent flyer. Maybe you've sat next to one of these guys who is so prepared that you feel like you don't know a thing about traveling. He's got the compact, lightweight carry-on that fits underneath his seat so that its contents are easily accessible throughout the flight. He has the little airport power adapter so his laptop never runs out of battery. He has the expensive noise-cancelling headphones so that he can enjoy his iPod and his mini-DVD player without being distracted by the low rumble of the plane's engines. Maybe the thing I'm the most jealous of is the little inflatable horseshoe pillow thing that goes around his neck so that he can comfortably fall asleep in an otherwise uncomfortable chair. They sell them in airports, but it seems like I only think about buying one after the flight. Then I think I'll remember to buy it before my next flight and I never do.

Been There, Done That

You know a frequent flyer when you see one. They've been around the block a few times. They know what they're doing. They're in it to win it. It's not that they enjoy traveling any more than the next guy does; they've simply accepted the fact that it's a part of life. They've decided that they are going places and they plan on making the most of the journey.

Are you a frequent flyer in student ministry? When people look at your day-to-day life, the way you travel from point A to point B, do they see you making the most of the experience? Maybe you don't love the fact that you're busy or that you have a million details to think about, but you recognize that they are the means to an end. If you're like most youth pastors, you probably love teenagers and want to make a difference in their lives. That sounds simple enough, but the reality is that if you're going to make that impact, if you're going to experience success in student ministry, you're going to have to deal with the day-in, day-out details that go into bringing that vision to pass.

One of the things that distinguishes a frequent flyer from the rest of the pack is the fact that they plan ahead. When you're on the move, you have to live your life intentionally. It's great if you pack all of the right things (and I hope that you have), but the real question is whether or not you'll use them effectively on the road. This is where I see a lot of youth leaders drop the ball. They have so much going for them. They've left the junk behind. They've packed everything they need to succeed. They've got the security of authority and accountability in their life. But when the rubber meets the road, they let day-to-day details keep them from being effective.

It's great if you have spiritual character, for example, but if you don't manage your schedule wisely you won't have much time to share it with others.

I hope that you have a loyal heart, and I know that your pastor will appreciate it, but if you don't develop your people skills, that reality may get lost in translation. Being a frequent flyer has less to do with theory and more to do with technique. It's not the "what"; it's the "how."

The best way for you to become an experienced frequent flyer is to experiment and to figure out what works best for you in your daily routine. There are plenty of resources out there that can help you go deep on any of the following topics. My goal here is to give you some practical direction that will get you started in the right direction. By paying attention to the following areas, you can increase your effectiveness, living and leading like a frequent flyer.

1. Pray Through the Day

I view each day as a gift from God, an opportunity to bring Him glory by accomplishing His will. Every day is an assignment and I have the privilege of partnering with Christ to carry that assignment out. That's why I start every day in prayer and it's why I pray about my entire day specifically before I ever leave the house. I pray through every appointment, that God would make His plan clear and that He would bless those I meet with. I pray for every potential opportunity, that God would order my steps and make His will apparent. I pray for the time I'll spend with my family. And because I know that there's no way I could anticipate everything that will happen, I pray for protection, wisdom, favor, direction, help, and strength.

On occasion, I'll pray a Scripture as it relates to the day ahead. One of my all-time favorite passages to pray is the apostle Paul's prayer for his disciples in Colosse (Colossians 1:9-14). I pray Paul's prayer over my life and over the lives of those I'll be interacting with that day, that we might be filled with the knowledge of God's will through all spiritual wisdom and understanding, that we might live a life worthy of the Lord, pleasing Him in every way, bearing fruit in every good work. This rich prayer continues and insightfully delineates those things we need to live for God from day to day.

The cool thing about praying through your day is that it opens your eyes to God's working throughout the day. More times than not, I sense the Lord at work in ways that I wouldn't be attentive to otherwise, except that I had taken the time to pray specifically about my day. It's also a lot more natural to "pray continually" throughout your day when your heart is sensitive to what God is doing in and through you (1 Thessalonians 5:17).

2. Get Organized

Being organized is one of the best ways you can help yourself as a frequent flyer. If you're going to be effective, you've got to have a grasp on what's going on in your life, when it needs to be done, and how it's going to get done.

As a leader, you need to be in control of your life on a very practical level.

In my opinion, there's no perfect system out there for being organized. At different times on my journey, I've had friends or mentors suggest one organizational system or another, trying to sell me on its benefits, explaining why I can't live without it. What I've come to discover is that there's no shortage of great systems out there. The important thing is determining which one is right for you. Find a system that makes sense in your mind and will work in your daily routine. A good organizational system should help you capture, process, prioritize, and execute all of the various "inputs" in your life, from projects to tasks, correspondence to appointments and everything in between.

When it comes to organization, keep in mind that your system will vary depending on your situation. If you're flying solo, you may take one approach, whereas an entirely different system may be required when you're working with a secretary or staff.

3. Manage Your Time

One of the areas where I'm continually striving to be intentional is time management. The reality for most of us is that there are more things to do, more people to see, and more places to go than hours in the day (or the week for that matter). I think it's important to recognize that and to have realistic expectations. There are plenty of resources out there to help you manage your time effectively or to maximize your productivity, but from my experience, you start managing your time by managing your expectations.

Strive for balance, but remember that perfect balance is elusive;

it doesn't exist in our imperfect world. When you have realistic expectations it makes ministry a lot easier. So when you see very little of your family for four days in a row, you don't panic, because you know that things get crazy from time to time. But then you take more time than usual with your family the following week. Stop looking for the perfect schedule because it doesn't exist. Come to grips with your busyness and recognize that it could be a lot worse. After all, there are a lot heavier crosses to bear than having to discipline your use of time.

I would encourage you to look at your time on the basis of stewardship. Ultimately, your time isn't really your time. It's God's, so don't squander it. Usually time isn't in hour-long segments. It's wasted minute by minute: checking the news online every 30 minutes, socializing with co-workers, dawdling around rather than doing what you know you're supposed to do. Staying up later than you should will result in less-than-peak performance the next day. It's one thing to complain about not having time for your family because you're diligently pouring your life out in sacrificial service; it's another thing when the reason you don't have time for your family is because you're a slacker or you have a habit of staying up late playing Nintendo Wii.

4. Work Well With Others

Another area where you should be intentional is in your interaction with those around you. As leaders, most of us have a team. You may have a dream team of full-time staff, a cadre of committed volunteers, or a handful of random helpers who don't know a thing about student ministry. I've worked with all of the above and everything in between and one of the things I've learned from my experience is that you shouldn't lead everyone the same. Everyone you work with has a different personality. Each individual brings a unique skill set to the team. Each one is motivated differently. And each one of them has a unique set of expectations for you as their leader.

Some would like you to walk them through every step of every project and enjoy talking at length about all of the details associated with each step. Others are self-sufficient and do better if you give them space. You may have one guy who could run your student ministry for weeks at a time in your absence. No one would notice you were gone. And you may have another leader that you wouldn't trust to watch the neighborhood's stray dog for 15 minutes. One of your leaders needs to be recognized for their accomplishments publicly to feel valued. Another one crawls under a rock when you say their name from the microphone.

Your challenge as the leader is to figure out the most effective way to lead the various people on your team.

I want to encourage you not to apply a one-size-fits-all approach to team leadership; it's easier up front, but in the end it's far less effective. When you're leading people, you want to bring out their best for the sake of the cause. That means from time to time you're going to have to challenge them or confront them or encourage them. The difficulty for you as the leader is in knowing when to do what. When do you kick them in the pants and when do you pat them on the back? There's a balance. You want to raise the bar and push the people on your team to do something truly great, and yet you don't want to dishearten them when what they offer is truly less than great. You want to motivate them without manipulating them. You want to stretch them without breaking them. This is more of an art than a science; there aren't hard-and-fast rules. You have to know the leaders on your team.

You also have to know what's going on in their lives. I might simply encourage a leader who dropped the ball when normally I would confront him, simply because I know that he's dealing with a significant personal challenge, or because I know he's juggling a couple of other things I've asked him to handle over and above his commitment.

5. Take Time for Yourself

An important part of leading intentionally is knowing when to step back from your work. It will still be there when you come back. Trust me on that one. When you're living out of your suitcase, you need time to regroup and to rest. You need time off, time with your family, time with your friends.

There is such wisdom in honoring the Sabbath. When you step away from your work and allow God to refresh you, you position yourself to finish it more effectively and efficiently when you come back to it. There have been times when I tried to keep working, when I really should've stopped and rested. I spent hours on something even though I wasn't getting any traction. When I came back to it after resting, everything seemed to fall into place. Pick a day off. Guard it. Don't answer your phone. Don't open your email. Don't think about work. When you honor the Sabbath, you'll come back to work ready for the day's challenges.

Sometimes a day off isn't enough, which is why it's important that you use your vacation time wisely.

A lot of times, we come back from vacation needing a vacation.

Spend your breaks resting and doing things that refresh you; it will make a big difference when you resume your responsibilities.

There was a time in student ministry when I really needed a break. To be honest, I was at the edge of burnout. By God's grace, I was keeping up with my responsibilities, but instead of operating out of a love of God and His people, I was checking things off a list, just trying to keep my head above water. It got to a point where I was so fatigued, I knew I needed some time away to get refreshed and recalibrated. Fortunately, the timing was right for me to use my 30-day sabbatical that the church offers staff members after seven years. It was incredibly refreshing and I'm convinced it's what kept me from burning out.

If you find yourself in a place where you're numb spiritually, operating out of obligation, talk to your leader. I'm not talking about being tired; we all get tired, and that's why we have a day off. But if you're legitimately approaching burnout, you need to talk with your leader and you need to take a break. Whatever inconvenience it may cause, preserving your spiritual life, your family, and your ministry are worth it.

Beyond time off, I would challenge you to put disciplines in your life that will keep you healthy. This journey is a marathon, not a sprint; order your life in such a way that you'll be as effective as possible for as long as possible. You're a steward of the body God has given you; it's the temple of the Holy Spirit. Some of the most important disciplines you can incorporate into your life have to do with your physical health—diet, exercise, and rest.

Be careful about preaching self-control in your youth service only to meet the kids afterward at the burger joint to slam down "the double widow-maker" with super-sized fries and 44 ounces of Mountain Dew. Make time in your busy schedule for regular physical activity. Lift weights or take a walk or get busy with Tae-Bo. Do something to stay in shape. Make a habit of getting to bed at a decent hour. If you're going to be at your best, you need your rest.

A Little Bit Goes a Long Way

It's been said that "the devil is in the details." I don't know how theologically sound the phrase is, but it's a figure of speech that's based on truth. As a leader, you can have the best of intentions, and still not live up to your potential. There are a lot of little things in life that make a big difference, like what you do with your discretionary time, how you handle a conversation, or when you go to bed.

In leadership, good intentions aren't enough.

There's a difference between having good intentions and being intentional, and ultimately, that difference is very practical.

You've packed your bag and made it this far, you may as well become a frequent flyer. It will make the rest of your journey all the more enjoyable and effective.

losing your luggage

My wife, Casey, started writing a book to encourage teenage girls when she was in high school and continued to work on it through her college years. *A Girl's Life with God* was published shortly after we were married. When Casey first started working on her manuscript, she didn't have a computer. Everything was written out by hand and there was no backup copy. On one fateful international flight, the airline lost Casey's luggage and with it—you guessed it—her nearly-complete manuscript. Usually, the airline is able to track down your luggage when they lose it, managing to send it on the next incoming flight. This was not the case for my wife, God bless her. The luggage never resurfaced and she had to start the book over from scratch. As I write this book, I have a new appreciation for what that must have felt like.

Few things are as aggravating as losing your luggage. You plan, you prepare, you pack, and are expecting a great trip, when your perfect plan is interrupted by something beyond your control. Maybe you can relate. You're having a great journey in student ministry, things seem to be going well, and then the unexpected happens: the outdoor outreach you've been planning all year is rained out, or the student you've worked so hard to reach goes off the deep end, or your worship leader quits, you find yourself in a financial crisis, or your church splits, or you lose a loved one, or you find yourself fighting a disease. It wasn't supposed to turn out this way. You feel like you've had the rug pulled right out from beneath your feet.

When you lose your luggage, you can't count on your planning, however pretty on paper it is. You have to improvise and you have to lead. When the unexpected happens, you've got to make do with what you've got—even if it's the clothes on your back and the $25 Food Court voucher the airline gave you for your inconvenience.

Flying by the Seat of Your Pants

When I think of lost luggage I think about one of our missions trips. You'll recall that we were going to Jamaica to serve a missionary during the day and hold evangelistic services in the evenings. The first leg of our trip went smoothly, all 58 of us arriving in Kansas City, excited about what God was going to do. But 30 minutes before we were supposed to board our next flight, our gate agent announced that our plane had a mechanical problem and paged me to the desk. She explained that the only available plane was smaller than the one we were supposed to be taking and that the only solution was to split our group up on two separate flights. Adamantly opposed to the idea, I wanted to keep everyone together, but she was eager to get the 58 of us out of her hair and insisted that there wasn't another option.

My associate took 18 students to New York City, I was routed with the 40 remaining students through Miami. We were told that we would be staying the night in our respective locations and would be put on the first available flights to Kingston in the morning.

When I arrived in Miami, I called my associate who was with the New York City group. I struggled to hear him over the bickering of the Miami students. He and his students had just gorged themselves at their 5-star hotel's all-you-can-eat buffet, compliments of the airline. They knew they wouldn't be eating like kings in Jamaica, so they stuffed themselves with filet mignon, king crab legs and every other culinary delicacy they could imagine. Dessert, anyone? No problem. What would you like? After dinner they went back to incredible rooms, plush with every imaginable amenity. Let's just say the New York City team rested well on their pillow-top mattresses before leisurely catching their mid-morning flight to Jamaica.

It was another story in Miami. We got in late and our flight out was going to be early. The airline arranged for us to stay in a hotel that was completely booked up. The attendant at the hotel was kind enough to make room for us, which meant that we had to stay in rooms that were closed for repair or had yet to be cleaned. Because there were only a handful of rooms available, we had up to six students sleeping in each room. For dinner that night, the 40 of us subsisted on stale granola bars, gifts from our friends at the airline. The students were hungry and exhausted and they let me know it. Our short night in Miami could not have gone by more slowly.

I was never more excited to get on an airplane to a third-world country than I was that next morning.

We asked the New York City kids to speak nothing of their pampering to the haggard Miami crew. But these were teenagers and someone broke their vow of silence. I spent much of the missions trip trying to rebuild the team unity that we left in the Kansas City airport.

Get a Grip

So what do you do when you lose your luggage? How do you lead when things don't go your way, or when it feels like your world is falling apart? Do you panic? Do you quit? Do you speed-read the latest seven-easy-steps self-help book from your favorite TV preacher? Do you call a friend?

The key to leading through crisis is perspective. Slow down, take a deep breath, and regain your perspective. It may feel like your everything is crashing down around your feet, but as a Christian, the foundation you've built your life on is firm. God is still on the throne and He knows where to find your luggage. He'll resolve things in His time. In the meantime, He's wanting to work in and through you.

Most of the time, the loss of your luggage is beyond your control. There's nothing you can do to prevent it or change it. There are some things you can do, however, before and during the crisis to help you maintain perspective.

1. Expect the Crisis

Jesus told us to expect difficulty in life (John 16:33). It's not a question of if we'll encounter crises, it's a question of when. Everyone faces great challenges at various points in their life. As leaders in ministry, we have the privilege of sharing some of people's happiest moments and many of their hardest ones. As I write this, I'm one week removed from multiple crises. Last week started at the hospital where I met a student who had attempted suicide; throughout the week I was dealing with two suspected cases of abuse; following our senior high service, I spoke with a handful of students whose lives are being ravaged by sin; and to top it all off, I ended the week by dismissing one of our volunteer leaders. As if that wasn't enough, all week long my entire family was fighting off what I'm convinced was some form of the bubonic plague. It was not a fun week.

Don't get me wrong; I'm not a pessimist. Actually, I'm an optimist and tend to see the glass as half full. I love it when things go well and prefer that they do, but I've been around long enough to know that there are going to be challenges and bumps along the road.

Paranoia isn't the answer, but when you expect the crisis, it's a lot easier to keep your perspective and to know that this too shall pass.

2. Grow Through the Crisis

One of the things that makes difficult times a bit easier to swallow is the fact that God uses them to strengthen our character, solidify our commitment, and to teach us lessons we might not learn otherwise. In fact, James encourages us to view our trials as "pure joy," because ultimately they are part of the process of our becoming mature (1:2). Keep that in perspective, because it's easy to get wrapped up in the details of your specific challenge, neglecting the fact that God is wanting to use it to strengthen you.

Specifically, James says that the testing of our faith develops perseverance.

In other words, hard times teach us to carry on.

If there's one thing I've learned in student ministry, it's that you have to stick with it. When everyone else is quitting, carry on. When you don't think you can go another mile, carry on. When you feel overworked and underappreciated, carry on. In the moment, it may feel like the hardest thing in the world to do, but James teaches us that it's the best thing you can do. Let perseverance finish its work so that you can be mature and complete, not lacking anything.

3. Share the Load

It's important that you have someone who will help you keep perspective. We all need someone we can unload our thoughts to or share our hearts with, especially in times of difficulty. There's something healing about being heard. If you're married, your spouse can help share the load. It could be a good friend, your accountability partner, or another staff member at your church.

I'm blessed to have a handful of people that help share the load in my life. I think particularly of Adam DeVizia and Scott Wiskus, good friends and staff at Realife. I can't tell you how many times over the years I've sat and just downloaded with one of them. Whether it's a few minutes between meetings or a couple of hours after a service, they're always willing to listen and I always value their perspective. We all need friends and family who, from time to time, will help us process life as it happens.

You need other people. Don't try to handle trials on your own; share the load.

4. Don't Overreact

One of the things I've noticed over the years is how easy it is to overreact when things aren't going well. I think of Jake, a high school student who was saved at Realife several years ago. At the time, I was leading a small group and Jake had just started attending. He had just given his life to Christ in one of our services and I had really been challenging him along with the rest of our students to be bold sharing their faith at school.

I was single at the time and it wasn't uncommon for students to stay at my house for a while after the meeting ended. One night, Jake was hanging around after small group and I could tell he wanted to talk.

"How's it going, Jake?" I asked.

"Alright, Pastor Scotty, but I need to talk with you about something."

"That's cool, Jake," I replied, "What's up?"

"Well, I don't even really want to mention this, but I feel like I should …" Jake struggled to get the words out and avoided eye contact.

"Listen, man, I'm your youth pastor, you can talk to me. What's going on?"

"Well, it's about school."

"What's going on at school?" I pressed for more information.

"I'm in trouble," Jake replied generically.

"OK …" I replied, wondering where the conversation might be going.

"And the police are involved."

"Listen, Jake, this is going to be a lot easier if you'll just tell me."

"Well, I was really excited about becoming a Christian last week. And I've been taking my Bible to school like you said we should. I've been telling people that I'm not the same anymore, but there's this guy that's been giving me a really hard time."

"So, what happened?" I asked.

"Well, he was bothering me all week. Finally, I got so frustrated that I decided to send him a message."

"And how did you do that?" I wondered aloud.

"I wrote 'Jesus loves you' on the side of his car ... with my key."

When things aren't going well, it's easy to overreact, as Jake did with his innovative, but ineffective evangelistic endeavor. I remember standing there listening to Jake, wondering what he had been thinking. That wasn't what I had in mind when I told our students to be bold in sharing their faith. Although there was a part of me that wanted to overreact as Jake's leader, I managed to stay calm. Everything worked out ... eventually. On top of it all, Jake grew through the experience, adding knowledge to his zeal for sharing the gospel.

While some crises will resolve themselves if they're left alone, others will require us to be a part of the solution as leaders. When possible, I've found it's best not to make any important decisions or take any major actions until things calm down and you've had a chance to gain perspective. Some situations, however, will require your immediate action. There are occasions where I have to intervene when a student is being abused in the home. When that's the case, I don't have the luxury of sitting around and gaining perspective. There have been times where we've had serious medical emergencies. In those instances, my only option as a leader is to act. When it is time to act, respond to the situation proportionately. Don't overreact.

On the Road Again

If you haven't already lost your luggage once or twice in student ministry, the day is coming when you will. When it happens, don't lose your perspective. Remember that God works all things together for good, even the crises (Romans 8:28).

God is at work in you and He wants to work through you, even in the difficult times. You may wish you could move on to the next milestone, but for whatever reason, God is asking you to stay put for a season. Wait it out; sooner or later, your luggage will surface and you'll be back on the road.

repacking your bag

As you travel from one milestone to the next on your journey, things will change. You will change. Your settings will change. Your role will change. From time to time, you'll need to repack your bags to keep up with it all. Certain milestones and transitions provide a natural opportunity to evaluate the contents of your bag and to make adjustments.

It's amazing how much stuff we can accumulate over time. We have a tendency to collect things on our journey, throwing them into the bag without thinking about whether or not we want to lug it around for the next 50 miles. Before long, the bag gets heavy and it's time to take everything out, determine what is really needed, throw some things out, and put some things back. In the process, you'll also make room for things you need to add for the next leg of your journey.

At some point, you may have witnessed the ultimate in repacking projects, which occurs occasionally with a woman and her purse. The first time I watched Casey unpack her purse, I was left speechless. It was like watching a magician pull item after increasingly outrageous item from his top hat. She started by pulling out the usual suspects—her wallet, some makeup, and various keys. Then came the pens and the notebook and the pictures. About the time I thought she was done, I realized she was just getting started. She found notes I had written her years ago, items she thought were lost, and the occasional Nutri-Grain wrapper. I was just waiting for her to whip out the white rabbit and the chain saw.

If you're not periodically repacking your bags, you won't be able to keep up with all that God is wanting to do in and through you.

Since you're going new places as a leader, you're going to have to repack.

Growing Pains

My ultimate destination has never changed, but I've spent the last 15 years in student ministry packing and repacking my bags for the next leg of my journey. I'm still carrying the essentials, but

I'm using a completely different set of resources today than I did when I started. It takes one set of resources to lead a group of 12 students. It takes something entirely different to balance weekly ministry to 1,000 students, directing 200 volunteer leaders, leading a departmental staff of eight, regularly preaching to the whole congregation as part of the church's preaching team, traveling to encourage youth leaders across the country, to say nothing about a whole lot of meetings and this little thing I have going on at home called "a family."

I don't give those references to draw attention to myself, but to draw a contrast between where I started and where I am today, and to point out that the journey has had a major learning curve and has required me to repack more times than I could count. I distinctly remember preaching one Wednesday night and realizing as I did that I no longer recognized all of the students. Until that point, I could tell you every student's name and a little bit about each of them. I drove home feeling guilty. *A good youth pastor would know all of their kids' names*, I thought. But it occurred to me later, as I tried to fall asleep, that I would have to repack. We were going somewhere I'd never been before, and I would need to rethink the way I traveled. It wasn't that I was the worst youth pastor; it was that I needed to start to develop a team of leaders who could help me make sure that each student was being cared for.

Several years later, I had a similar experience with our volunteer leadership team. A college student introduced himself to me. I didn't recognize him, so I asked if it was his first week serving at Realife. He informed me that he'd been helping out for six months. Same song, different verse; I drove home that night feeling miserable. I wondered how I could effectively lead students if I didn't even know the leaders who were helping us do so. It required rethinking and repacking, and as a result, we lead our volunteers differently today than we did back then.

If you're going to grow your student ministry, you're going to have to rethink things from time to time.

This fact may encourage some and discourage others, but the reality is that you'll never have a perfect plan or system. Just about the time you think you get something figured out, you're going to have to tweak it or change it to accommodate the growth God is adding to your group or to address needs that come to your attention.

Our volunteer leadership team is a great example of that fact. More than any other area, we're continually evaluating the organization and use of our volunteer leaders, because it affects everything else we do. The health and growth of every program we run depends on the effectiveness of our leadership team. Our ability to effectively disciple young people is directly correlated to the health of our volunteer leadership team.

Over the years, we've gone through more leadership structures than I can probably remember, but we don't change for the sake of change. Each of our approaches was appropriate for where we were at the time. If you're paying attention, there are moments in ministry where, as a leader, you sense something needs to change. That's when it's time to repack.

As a church, we've repacked several times. We started renting space in a couple of storefronts before moving to a skating rink. When we outgrew that, we repacked and moved to our first building. It wasn't long, though, before we were repacking again, this time to make room for a major building expansion. After a few more years, we moved down the highway to our current facility, but we continue to unpack and repack. About a year or so after we moved to our current facility, we built the Realife Student Center. As I write this book, we're about to expand it to make room for all that God is doing today.

In addition to all of the thought and energy we've spent repacking physically, we've gone through all kinds of shifts in our programming and approaches to ministry. All of the countless changes over the years have required me to adjust on occasion in order to be as effective as possible.

Evaluation Station

We're continually evaluating everything we do at Realife. If you do the same things over and over again, you should naturally get better and better at doing them. To me, there's nothing more frustrating than making the same mistake twice.

Maybe you couldn't have avoided the mistake the first time around, but there's no excuse for making it the second or third time around.

And the only way to ensure that you won't make those mistakes is to effectively make evaluation a part of your leadership.

Evaluation isn't difficult, but it takes discipline. It takes discipline because it's an exercise that you won't see the benefits of immediately. Evaluation is a discipline that will benefit you and your ministry over the long haul.

The best time to do an evaluation is when the event or program you're evaluating is still fresh on your mind. The temptation after the big event is to crash. Don't—your work isn't done yet. The event or the program isn't over until the evaluation has been completed. Get an evaluation from everyone who was involved in the project, rather than relying solely on your own observations. You probably have a variety of leaders on your team with a variety of perspectives; many of them will observe things you never thought about.

Everyone's evaluations should be submitted in writing. Next, they should be reviewed and compiled into one document. When you're allowing multiple people to submit evaluations you're going to get some conflicting observations. One person thought the human video to Carman's "This Blood" was so life-changing it should become a staple of every single youth service. Another observer adamantly argues that you should never do another human video ever again. You can allow discussion on the matter, but as the leader, you have to ultimately decide which direction you're going to go. The final decision on the matter should be reflected in the final copy of the evaluation, which should be filed for next time.

The next time you're going to hold an outreach, the first thing you should do is pull out the notes from the last time. This is critical. You may think you'll remember everything from the last event, but you won't. Trust me. I would also encourage you to review your evaluation a few different times throughout the event planning process.

You could evaluate everything from your youth service to your small group program to your outreach events and beyond. Occasionally, we'll even survey students or hold a focus group to add to our evaluations. When you're involving students and leaders in an evaluation process, it's important that you establish and foster a constructive environment. Be careful not to create a forum for people to get together and complain about what they'd like you to do differently. If you'll develop a healthy culture of evaluation, one that's based on unity and goodwill, you'll develop a culture of improvement. Year after year, you'll find yourself becoming increasingly effective.

In addition to the benefits it will bring to your ministry, evaluation can help you grow personally. For the last several years, I've made a habit of giving my close friends and co-workers a form to use in evaluating my effectiveness as a leader. The document has about 25 questions and covers a variety of topics from my effectiveness as a leader to my effectiveness as a communicator to how good a friend I've been.

I offer this suggestion with some caution. I only recommend proceeding with this kind of personal evaluation if you trust the hearts of those you ask to participate. You also should respect their discernment and ability to give constructive criticism that is fair-minded. Be careful about who you open your life and leadership to at this level of scrutiny. Proverbs says that the "wounds of a friend can be trusted" (27:6). It may not feel good to have someone point out your weaknesses, but if they are a true friend, you'll be better for it.

When I hand my personal evaluation out, I ask my friends to be brutally honest. I appreciate their encouragement throughout the year, but in an evaluation, I'm not looking for affirmation or a pat on the back. I want honest feedback that's going to help me identify areas where I need to grow. The first few times I read over the team's evaluations, I learned quite a bit about myself and about the team. Now, after doing it for several years, I'm not nearly as surprised by some of the answers, because I know where I'm strong and where I'm weak. Yet, by tracking my evaluations from year to year, I'm able to gauge my growth over time by comparison.

I made a lot of mistakes early on in student ministry; I'm just glad I left room in my carry-on for all the lessons I learned as a result.

You don't have to have it all figured out, just leave room in your carry-on for improvement.

When to Repack

So how do you know when it's time to repack? When your bag is getting too heavy to carry, there's a good chance something needs to go. There are busy seasons, but if you find yourself completely buried under your responsibilities, it may be time to simplify.

In 2003, we had a sense that we were carrying too heavy a load as a ministry. Our staff and leaders were tired, some at the point of burnout, and many of our students were overwhelmed by all of the competing programs we were throwing their way. So we looked closely at the entire ministry from top to bottom. The Realife Revolution was about simplifying what we did and focusing on doing those things well. We let good programs die to make room for the right ones. We worked hard to ease the load on our volunteers and we evaluated our own leadership as a staff. As a ministry and as individuals, we sensed that our suitcases were getting heavy and it was time to repack.

Times of transition are also natural times to repack your bags. If you're adding or losing staff, you probably should consider repacking. If you're making major changes to your youth service or your programs, you should probably think about how that's going to affect your leadership. As you hit different growth points numerically, you'll probably sense that certain transitions need to be made in your approach and those will necessitate an evaluation of what you're doing as a leader at that time.

From time to time, when you repack, you'll get rid of everything that can be eliminated and may still feel like there's not enough room for everything you need to carry. If that's the case, you may need to get a bigger bag.

From time to time, God will stretch you and ask you to carry more than you think you can handle.

Cooperate with God in the process. Before you know it, you'll look back at the things you think are hard now and laugh at how easy they seem by comparison to where you'll be (hopefully that's encouraging and not discouraging).

How to Repack

It's important to repack in the right way. Here are some tips to help you make the most of the experience:

1. The Right Time

There is a right and a wrong time to repack. Choose a time when you'll be able to devote your undivided attention to the task. For example, if your youth service is Wednesday night, Wednesday morning is probably the wrong time. If you're in the midst of an important or sizable project requiring a significant amount of your attention, it's probably best to wait until it's been completed. When you start the repacking process, be sure to block out a large amount of time to allow you to do so adequately and thoroughly, without interruption. If you're doing a major overhaul, repacking could take the better part of a day. At other times, you may be able to get the job done in 30 minutes. The amount of time will depend on how much you're unpacking and repacking.

2. The Right Place

The right place is also important. I've found it's good to get away from the office so that I'm not distracted by the million other things that are clamoring for my attention. If there's a lot happening at your house, it may not be the best choice either. Choose a place where you can relax and have the space to spread everything out. It's a rare treat when I can get away for a day or two to repack. Usually, I'm thinking, organizing, and planning at my home office. You may have a favorite spot to get away and think. Or, maybe one of your church members has offered to let you use their lake house. The important thing is that you're not distracted, so find the right place to repack.

3. The Right Tools

You'll want access to your calendar and any important information relevant to whatever it is you're repacking. For instance, if you're focusing on your personal life, you may need little more than your calendar, a Bible and a pen and paper. If you're focusing on repacking your ministry, you may also need a list of your programs or leaders. If at all possible, shut your phone off to minimize distractions and interruptions during the process.

4. The Right Approach

I would encourage you to seek God's help in the repacking process, rather than trying to figure it out on your own. Start by reading a relevant passage of Scripture or praying. Occasionally, pause to pray about the ideas you're having and to ask the Lord to continue to direct the process. Then write everything out; get all of the factors that you're dealing with on the table. If I was processing my schedule, for example, I would write down all of my existing commitments and I'd write down everything I needed to add to my calendar. Then, I would begin problem-solving, deciding what could be eliminated or delegated. In some cases, I may need to make a sacrifice in one area to make room for something else. Or I may need to entirely rethink my approach to, say, team leadership or sermon planning so that it will fit back into the suitcase.

Often, when repacking, I'll run my plan by a few people whose feedback I respect and trust. Chances are, you have a good idea of what needs to happen, but sharing your plan with an objective person outside of your situation may help you see some things you missed or spur other ideas. There have been times I thought I needed to hold on to something, but a good friend helped me to see that I could let go of it. At other times, I've been encouraged by someone to bring something along for the journey that I might not have thought of otherwise.

The goal is that, by the end of your time, you're able to make some decisions. What will you throw out? What will you replace? What needs to be changed or downsized? What needs to be added? Once you've made those decisions, the last step is determining what changes you'll need to make in order for those things to happen.

Repacking may take some work, but if you're anything like me, you'll experience a huge sense of relief once it's done! As great as that is, the really exciting thing is that repacking prepares you to be even more effective, both now and in the future.

10

leaving room

Socrates said that "the unexamined life isn't worth living." His conclusion is a bit strong, but his premise is true. Life loses much of its richness when we fail to stop and reflect, connecting the day-to-day details of our lives with the bigger picture. It's unfortunate, but a lot of youth leaders I talk with have a sort of tunnel vision. I admire their focus, but they don't take time to look around them on the journey. If they would, they'd realize there are all kinds of things they could pick up on the way and put into their suitcase.

They travel from point A to point B, from one event to the next, from this meeting to that one. They are busy collecting all of the latest ideas, reading all of the latest books, talking to all kinds of important people. Their schedules are full. Their minds are racing.

The last thing they're interested in doing is stopping to reflect. After all, they think, why look back when you can move forward?

As a youth pastor in a fast-paced environment, I've gained an appreciation for the little opportunities God gives me to reflect, whether it's 15 minutes at Jiffy Lube while I'm getting my oil changed or it's the lull after a big event. If you will take the time to stop and think about the most recent leg of your journey, you'll find all kinds of things you can pack for the road ahead—lessons learned and souvenirs of God's faithfulness.

Life Lessons

Leave plenty of room in your suitcase for the lessons you're going to learn on your student ministry journey. You'll remember from the first chapter that I've made my fair share of ministry mistakes. A lot of them were the result of my ignorance. As disappointing as they can be, mistakes are understandable (in fact, they are to be expected) when you lack understanding or experience. Making the same mistakes over and over again is less understandable and will keep you from experiencing success in student ministry.

As a spiritual leader, I hope that you're a lifelong learner. Life is a great teacher. By simply paying attention to what's happening all around you, you'll get quite the education. Maintain a teachable spirit and you'll see all kinds of opportunities for improvement, whether you're observing the successes and failures of others from a distance or evaluating your own, up close and personal.

When things go well, don't get cocky and take for granted that they always will. Make notes of what you learn from the experience. Instead of getting frustrated when things don't go your way, take a minute to honestly and objectively ask why that's the case. We discussed the discipline of evaluation in the last chapter, and I hope that you'll incorporate it into your life and ministry. Be sure to leave room in your carry-on so you make the most of the experience.

Significant Souvenirs

In addition to all the lessons you're going learn along the way, you need to leave room in your student ministry suitcase for souvenirs from the journey. God wants us to look forward, especially as leaders, but He wants us to do so with an appreciation for what's past. All too easily we forget what God has done in our hurry to the next big thing. Or, worse yet, we forget that God is the one who's done the work and try to take some credit for ourselves.

If you don't guard your heart in ministry, you can lose your sense of wonder about the fact that God is the one ultimately at work in your ministry.

When you begin to understand the inner workings of the ministry, the behind-the-scenes details that go into the youth service or the event or the small group program, it's easy to reduce the work of

God to mechanics—this leader doing this, using this approach, based on this principle, producing this result. We begin to think that because we know how things work, we can make things happen and, as a result, we no longer marvel at God's mysterious working in and through us.

At first, it's easy to depend on God, because you're wet behind the ears and don't have a clue about what you're doing. But after you've been around the track a few times, you start to feel more comfortable, and if you're not careful, you no longer depend on God as you did in the early days.

As our competence increases, we have to be careful that our dependence on God doesn't decrease.

In the Old Testament, leaders would occasionally build monuments commemorating the work of God in their midst. There's wisdom in that approach. As the Israelites traveled back and forth, they would see those monuments and be reminded of God's involvement in their situation. It helped put things in perspective. God was the one who called them out of Egypt for His purposes; He was the one who drove out their enemies and gave them a good land as their inheritance. He fought their battles in the past and would do so in the future if they would only let Him.

From time to time, you should do the same thing—packing souvenirs that remind you of where you've been and what God has done. Take them with you as you travel in unfamiliar places.

Display them where you will see them. There are all kinds of ways to gather souvenirs, collecting an item that reminds you of something God did, writing about His moving in a journal, keeping a file of all of these things to look through when you're discouraged.

What to Collect

So what should you collect? Collect items that remind you that God is the one who is at work. You don't have to collect everything, but save those things that remind you of God's intervention in your situation. It could be your end-of-the-year giving statement showing that you exceeded the missions giving goal that you thought was impossible. It could be an encouraging note from a student that arrived after what you felt was a particularly terrible sermon. It might be a ticket from an event where God moved powerfully in the group as a result of your prayers.

A really practical thing you could collect would be photos and videos. I know of some youth leaders who create an end-of-the-year DVD with the best video footage and photography from the year. As much as the students love them, the project is really rewarding for the leader, as it gives them opportunity to reflect on all that God did in and through them that year in student ministry.

We need to be reminded that it's not up to us.

It's not our wisdom. It's not our strategy. It's not our creativity. It's not our ability to preach or to organize. God may use all of those things, but ultimately it's His supernatural wisdom and power that produce results.

You should also collect souvenirs that remind you what the journey is all about. Pack those items that remind you why you set out on this journey in the first place. The senior picture of the student who wouldn't have graduated high school without your help. The heart wrenching email from a student that brought tears to your eyes. The letter from the parent who used to give you a hard time, but now has seen a remarkable difference in the lives of their kids because of your ministry.

On my desk I have a picture of one of our past students. I remember pulling Ryan out of youth service as an out-of-control freshman. He was continually causing problems, distracting his friends from focusing on what God was doing in the service. My heart was broken for Ryan and his friends, and it got to the point where I was honestly fed up. We'd gone through the confrontation thing several times now and I was determined that this would be the last. His disrespect for leadership and the things of God was starting to affect the group.

We got out to the hallway and I didn't waste any time. "Listen Ryan, I'm doing everything I know to do to help you live for God, but if you're determined not to, my hands are tied. You can go to hell if you want to, but I'm not about to stand by while you take all of your friends with you! You can straighten up or you can stay at home, but I'm not going to let you disrupt what God is doing in our group."

From that day forward, Ryan began to change. Today, he's living for Jesus. As a matter of fact, he's flying a Blackhawk helicopter in Iraq and his faith in God is what keeps him strong. Recently, Ryan was featured in an article in *The New York Times*. As I read it, I was blown away thinking about how incredible his transformation has been and what an impact he's having as a result. Whenever Ryan's in town, he stops by my office to visit and catch me up on how God is working in his life. We stay in touch and he often thanks me for challenging him to live for God, confronting him with the truth.

I can't tell you how much it encourages me to see Ryan's picture on a day when it seems like nothing is going right, or when I'm dealing with a student who seems like he'll never change. I'm reminded that God is able to intervene; He's done it before and He'll do it again. All I have to do is trust Him.

Another souvenir I see regularly is Nathan Teegarden, Realife's high school director. He's a little too big to fit in my carry-on, but watching his life and leadership is a big encouragement. Nathan was saved at one of our outreach events as a high school student. As fun as it was to watch him grow in God through school and then college, what's been really incredible is having him join the staff. Nathan has been on the team for a little over a year now, and he's already making a tremendous impact on high school students. I'm convinced that some of them will one day be youth pastors making a difference just like Nathan. That's a pretty incredible souvenir!

I receive souvenirs every single day in the form of emails

from students and parents. Some break my heart. Others are encouraging. This email I recently received from a girl in our group did both:

"To give you some background, my family has been involved in alcohol or drugs throughout the majority of my life. I do not have a strong Christian influence at home, neither one of my parents hardly ever go to church and part of the time I have to fight one or both for me to go to church. Eight times out of ten I go home to someone screaming and yelling. Both of my parents have been divorced, remarried (each other) and have separately talked to me about divorcing again. I have also been violated by two different men. My family does not know about it because when I tried to tell them about the first one they didn't believe me and told me I was lying. The second violation being worse than the first, I repressed it and have only recently acknowledged that it did happen. Having almost completely lost my ability to trust men, let alone anyone, I shut myself off from the world.

"I began building up a great sense of pain, anger, and hatred toward all of those that had hurt me and was unable to tell anybody about my feelings. I entered a depression where more and more everyday I felt a piece of me taken, I felt like I was losing my mind. I entered a suicidal state where for about two years, maybe more, my thoughts circulated around my own death. I would spend my time thinking of the cleanest way to go about doing it, so when it was done the person that would have to clean up after me would not have a big mess. I only tried a couple of times, which thankfully did not succeed. Most times, I would curl up in my room crying, praying, begging for God to take me home to heaven.

"My inability to trust people affected my ability to trust God; in truth, I didn't trust at all. I started shutting off my emotions when I was around certain people and turning them back on later. One day they didn't come back on. I didn't want to feel the pain and hatred anymore, so I embraced the ultimate defense without God. I shut my emotions and my mind completely down to a point of no feeling. No pain, no anger, no hatred, no love, no purpose. I simply had no reason to get up in the morning. I virtually stopped eating, I was an empty shell. I walked and breathed but inside I was dead.

"Then one day I did something that I had never done. I dared to trust, not just anything or anybody, but God. I simply decided I was tired of everything and was going to try it His way. I began to get more involved in church. I joined choir and began handing my talents one by one to God's uses. A sense of freedom, a breath of fresh air consumed me. A hope restored, a purpose given, a self-respect and confidence gained, I no longer lived my life in the shadow of pain and despair. Though I still go home to just about the same situation, I do not carry the burdens I once had. Even when I didn't have a hold of God, God had a hold on me. He was the only one there, He is the only reason I'm still here. Now that I've gotten this far, I'll never go back. Never."

I receive emails like this regularly, reminders of why God has called me to impact this generation with real life in Jesus Christ. One of the reasons I leave room in my suitcase for souvenirs is because it's good to be reminded that what we do in student ministry is incredibly personal.

God is a personal God and He's working uniquely in the lives of real people.

Youth service isn't some show or production. Student ministry isn't about some event or program. It's about real people who need God's intervention in a personal way.

Room for Improvement

Whatever you pick up along the way in your student ministry journey, make sure you leave room for a little bit more. Some things have gotten easier the longer I've been in student ministry. When I no longer need something that's taking up space in the suitcase, I'll leave it behind to make room for another significant souvenir or life lesson, knowing I'll need them down the road.

Writing this book has given me a unique opportunity to reflect on 15 years in student ministry. Perhaps you've been in ministry longer than I have. Or, maybe you've just hit the road and haven't yet worked 15 days with teenagers. Wherever you are at on your journey, whatever your experience, I want you to think about the same question. What do you have to show for it? I'm not talking about results or status or even success. I'm asking about the contents of your suitcase. What do you have to show for the time you've spent working with young people? I hope it's more than a headache and a half-eaten box of pizza. What have you learned along the way? How have you grown? What has God done? How has He helped you? Whose life has been changed?

There's no way I could anticipate all that the next 15 years hold for me. I hope and pray that God continues to allow me to work with teenagers, introducing them to real life in Jesus Christ. Wherever the journey takes me, and however I get there, one thing's for sure. I'm going to bring my carry-on. And with it, countless memories, stories, experiences, and lessons—resources for the road ahead.

afterword

As I write the final words of this book, I look across the room at my carry-on. The top is open, partially packed for the next leg of my journey, the rest of its contents spread across my bed. In a matter of hours, I'll take another drive to the airport and another stroll through security before boarding another airplane so I can go speak to another group of students. I'm not doing it for the frequent flyer miles, nor am I addicted to the pretzels that comprise a mid-flight snack served at 30,000 feet. I'm not getting on another plane because I love to "fly the friendly skies." It's definitely not because of the luxurious leg room afforded me by the puddle-jumpers that service the Springfield airport.

I do it because God has called me to introduce students to real life in Jesus Christ.

One student at a time, God is allowing me to partner with Him to change history.

The student ministry journey is one of the most adventurous and rewarding I could ever imagine.

So, regardless of the challenges, the failures, and the adversity that sometimes causes me to wonder if it's even worth it, I persevere. I continue. I press forward. I carry on, considering my life "worth nothing to me, if only I may finish the race and complete the task the Lord Jesus has given me—the task of testifying to the gospel of God's grace" (Acts 20:24). What a privilege!

Thanks for allowing me to share my heart with you through this simple book. You've probably noticed by now that I haven't approached it as an expert, but as a fellow traveler trying to make a difference, faithfully fulfilling my calling. My hope is that you will pack and persevere for success in student ministry.

I leave you with words from the apostle Paul, a guy who knew a lot about traveling, packing, repacking, and finishing strong. The following verses sum up my own personal hope and my prayer for you on this journey:

"I'm not saying that I have this all together, that I have it made. But I am well on my way, reaching out for Christ, who has so wondrously reached out for me. Friends, don't get me wrong: By no means do I count myself an expert in all of this, but I've got my eye on the goal, where God is beckoning us onward—to Jesus. I'm off and running, and I'm not turning back. So let's keep focused on that goal, those of us who want everything God has for us. Now that we're on the right track, let's stay on it. Stick with me, friends. Keep track of those you see running this same course, headed for this same goal. We're citizens of high heaven! We're waiting the arrival of the Savior, the Master, Jesus Christ, who will transform our earthy bodies into glorious bodies like his own. He'll make us beautiful and whole with the same powerful skill by which he is putting everything as it should be, under and around him. My dear, dear friends! I love you so much. I do want the very best for you. You make me feel such joy, fill me with such pride. Don't waver.

Stay on track, steady in God" (Philippians 3:12-17, 20-21; 4:1, *The Message*).

Carry on,
Scotty Gibbons

about the author

Scotty Gibbons has been the director of Realife Student Ministries at James River Assembly since 1993. When he started, Scotty could drive the entire youth group around in a van. Today, the Realife Student Center is home to more than 1,000 students and 200 volunteer leaders.

Scotty is a nationally recognized youth communicator with a passion for reaching students and equipping leaders.

Scotty, his wife Casey, and their daughters live in Ozark, Missouri.

notes

notes

notes

notes

notes

notes